Socrates Meets Hume

Other Works of Peter Kreeft from St. Augustine's Press

Philosophy 101 by Socrates
Socrates Meets Descartes
Socrates Meets Freud
Socrates Meets Kant
Socrates Meets Kierkegaard
Socrates Meets Machiavelli
Socrates Meets Marx
Socrates Meets Sartre
The Philosophy of Jesus
Jesus-Shock
Summa Philosophica
Socratic Logic
Socrates' Children: Ancient
Socrates' Children: Medieval
Socrates' Children: Modern
Socrates' Children: Contemporary
Socrates' Children [all four books in one]
An Ocean Full of Angels
The Sea Within
I Surf, Therefore I Am
If Einstein Had Been a Surfer

Socrates Meets Hume

The Father of Philosophy Meets the Father of
Modern Skepticism

A Socratic Cross-Examination of Hume's
An Enquiry Concerning Human Understanding

By Peter Kreeft

ST. AUGUSTINE'S PRESS
South Bend, Indiana

Manufactured in the United States of America

1 2 3 4 5 6   20 19 18 17 16 15 14

Library of Congress Control Number: 2020935699

✕ The paper used in this publication meets the minimum requirements of
the American National Standard for Information Sciences Permanence of
Paper for Printed Materials, ANSI Z39.481984.

St. Augustine's Press
www.staugustine.net

Contents

Preface

This book is one in a series of Socratic explorations of some of the Great Books. Books in this series are short, clear, and nontechnical, thus fully understandable by beginners. They also introduce (or review) the basic questions in the fundamental divisions of philosophy: metaphysics, epistemology, anthropology, ethics, logic, and method. They are designed both for classroom use and for educational do-it-yourselfers. The "Socrates Meets . . ." books can be read and understood completely on their own, but each is best appreciated after reading the little classic it engages in dialogue.

The setting—Socrates and the author of the Great Book meeting in the afterlife—need not deter readers who do not believe there is an afterlife. For although the two characters and their philosophies are historically real, their conversation, of course, is not and requires a "willing suspension of disbelief". There is no reason the skeptic cannot extend this literary belief also to the setting.

Introduction

Hume is the most formidable, serious, difficult-to-refute skeptic in the history of human thought.

I will never forget my first exposure to him, in a seminar in Modern Philosophy at Calvin College taught by William Harry Jellema, who was the best teacher I ever had but who, like Socrates, never wrote a book. All ten of us in the seminar were philosophy majors and friends. We had to read Hume over vacation week. We took this great skeptic very seriously, because we were more concerned with finding the truth than with finding an A, and Hume deeply disturbed us because we could not refute his arguments, yet could not accept his skeptical conclusions. For if we did, what would become of philosophy? What would become of science and common sense and religion and morality and education and human knowledge in general? The whole process of liberation from the cave of ignorance would be merely another cave.

We shared our anguish with the professor when classes resumed, but instead of "telling us the answers", he simply sent us back to Hume again, with the reminder to remember our logic. If we did not accept Hume's conclusion, we had to find either an ambiguously used term, or a false premise, expressed or implied, or a logical fallacy. It was not sufficient simply to say we disagreed with his conclusion; we had to refute his argument.

That is the process you are invited to participate in, with the aid of Socrates.

No one *wants* to be a skeptic; no one is happy as a skeptic, except the unpleasant type who just want to shock and upset people. Happy skeptics are dishonest; unhappy skeptics are honest. (The same is true of atheists. Only idiots, masochists, or immoralists *want* to be atheists. Contrast Sartre, the happy hypocritical atheist, with Camus, the unhappy, honest atheist.) Hume is an unhappy skeptic, an honest skeptic, and he demands and deserves to be taken very seriously and answered very carefully.

He also deserves this because of his continuing, enormous influence on English-speaking philosophy today. Hume's immediate thought-child was the extreme, dogmatic, reductionistic form of "analytic philosophy" that called itself "logical positivism", as summarized in A. J. Ayer's *Language, Truth and Logic*. This is no longer in vogue, but softer, modified versions of it are, and they all go back to Hume, especially his reduction of all objects of human reason to "matters of fact" and "relations of ideas". These are approximately what Kant later called "synthetic a posteriori propositions" and "analytic a priori propositions". But please don't close this book and run when you see these verbal monsters. Hume uses a minimum of such technical terms and gives clear, common-sense definitions of each of them. Hume may be disturbing, and he may be disturbed, and he may even be dull sometimes (I tried to omit all the dull passages), but he is always clear.

Hume is also very important because of his influence on Kant and because of the influence of both

Hume and Kant on all subsequent philosophy. Kant says it was Hume who woke him from his "dogmatic slumber". And by his "Copernican revolution in philosophy", which was his answer to Hume, Kant divided the history of Western philosophy in two (the pre-Kantian and the post-Kantian) almost as Christ divided history into B.C. and A.D. (The next book in this series will be on Kant.)

Hume's philosophy, like that of Locke and Berkeley before him, is an Empiricist critique of the Rationalism of Descartes, "the father of modern philosophy". Hume's skeptical conclusions were the logical consequences of Locke's Empiricist starting point. They were conclusions that Locke did not draw because they were too radical. By his relationship to both his successors and his predecessors, Hume holds a crucial position in the history of Western philosophy, that "great conversation" that began with Socrates and is still going on.

The typical three-stage bare-bones summary of classical modern philosophy is: Descartes' Rationalism versus Hume's Empiricism versus Kant's Idealism. All three are theories in *epistemology*. Most of the philosophy in that astonishingly rich two-hundred-year period between the publication of Descartes' *Discourse on Method* in 1637 and the death of Hegel in 1831, the period of classical modern philosophy, was concerned with epistemology. "Epistemology" means "theory of knowledge". (What is knowledge? How do we know? How does it work? How *should* it work?) It is probably the trickiest and most purely theoretical division of philosophy. Yet it is foundational, for any position you take in epistemology will always have consequences for, and make a great deal of difference to, all the rest of your philosophy: your metaphysics, cosmology, philosophical theology, anthropology, ethics, and political philosophy.

Philosophers frequently write two versions of their thoughts, one long and the other short. Inevitably, the short book becomes the classic, the book that is well known and loved, while the longer one becomes the subject of advanced and abstruse doctoral dissertations. Descartes wrote the simple *Discourse on Method* as well as the more difficult *Meditations*. Kant wrote the relatively simple and short *Prolegomena to any Future Metaphysic* as well as the formidable and long *Critique of Pure Reason*. He also wrote the short and simple *Fundamental Principles of the Metaphysics of Morals* as well as the long and complex *Critique of Practical Reason*. Similarly, Hume wrote the short *Enquiry Concerning Human Understanding*[1] as well as the longer *Treatise on Human Nature*.

Like his readers, he preferred his shorter work. In fact he explicitly called his earlier, longer book "that juvenile work" in the preface to the posthumous 1777 edition of the later one (the *Enquiry*), adding: "Henceforth the Author desires that the following pieces may alone be regarded as containing his philosophical sentiments and principles."

This book is a short Socratic critique of Hume's short classic, the *Enquiry Concerning Human Understanding*, in the form of a Socratic dialogue between the two philosophers who meet after death.

---

[1] Texts quoted from Hume's *Enquiry Concerning Human Understanding* are indicated as E in the sidenotes.

In quoting Hume's words, I have altered some of the punctuation, since eighteenth-century English style multiplied commas in a way that appears bewildering and confusing to twenty-first-century readers.

I have sometimes italicized Hume's words for emphasis. The student can refer to Hume's texts in order to differentiate.

I have also capitalized "Empiricism" and "Rationalism", as two ideologies, but not "empiricistic" and "rationalistic", as two generic tendencies or methods.

I have at times ventured beyond Hume's actual words in imagining how he would have replied to some of Socrates' questions. I trust that I have not violated the integrity of Hume's philosophy in doing so, but I cannot guarantee this.

This is not a scholarly work. There are more exact, more technical, and more severely logical critiques of Hume, but I have deliberately used none of these professional secondary sources but only my own more "amateur", spontaneous, original ones, which I think are more simple and natural and commonsensical.

I have also compressed some of Socrates' arguments, rather than always having him use his famous "Socratic method" of long, careful, step-by-step questioning, when I thought the latter would become too tedious or artificial. My apologies to the real Socrates.

I

Hume Introduced

[SETTING: Somewhere after death.]

SOCRATES: David Hume! Is that you?

HUME: I . . . I think so.

SOCRATES: You're not certain?

HUME: I always was skeptical of that little word, "certain".

SOCRATES: In fact, you were even skeptical of that other little word, "I".

HUME: True. I denied the existence of a substantial self.

SOCRATES: Whom am I addressing, then? Or should I say "*Hume* am I addressing?" Is it at least a Humean being? A secular Humeanist, perhaps?

HUME: I suppose you are Socrates, and this is my Purgatory, and I am to be tortured with puns.

SOCRATES: How perceptive you are! The first two of your three suppositions are right. But I am not your torturer but your teacher, and my instruments will not be puns but probes, questions.

HUME: I seem to have no choice but to accept my fate. I think this will prove to be the most interesting dream I have ever had.

SOCRATES: It does not matter for now whether you believe this is a dream or reality, as long as you are willing to continue our conversation.

HUME: I hope I can remember it when I wake. Perhaps I will write it up and publish it as a book.

SOCRATES: But you are already in a book, which is being written by another even as we speak.

HUME: God, you mean?

SOCRATES: Goodness, no! Just a philosophy professor in the twenty-first century. We are characters in his book.

HUME: Oh, dear. As bad as all that, is it?

SOCRATES: Why are you so upset?

HUME: I distrust philosophy professors. Neither of *us* ever occupied that position, you know, Socrates, as most philosophers did. And I think we have other things in common too, notably your famous Socratic doubts.

SOCRATES: I did not begin with doubts, but with questions.

HUME: What is the difference?

SOCRATES: Questions hope to find answers.

HUME: Of course they do. What is your point?

SOCRATES: Your thought ended in skepticism; mine did not.

HUME: Ah, I see. But you *began* there, with doubts and questions. So we are spiritually akin there.

SOCRATES: In a sense, yes.

HUME: And because of that common skepticism, we were both misunderstood and feared by our contemporaries. We both upset people by questioning their thoughtless or confused prejudices, and they condemned us as their enemies, when in fact we both only wanted to be their friends by delivering them from superstitions and ignorance. Is that not so?

SOCRATES: Again I must answer: in a sense, yes.

HUME: You are here with me now for that reason, are you not? To be my friend rather than my enemy or my censor?

SOCRATES: Oh, yes. Unlike my disciple Plato in the *Republic*, I was suspicious of the censorship of ideas, just as you were, for I was the victim of it even more than you were. You were only denied a teaching position because of your ideas, but I was denied my life.

HUME: I am greatly relieved. I have read your dialogues with the Sophists, and I feared you were here to confound and refute me as you did them.

SOCRATES: Oh, I did not say that I was not here for that purpose. I only said I was not here to censor you. I did not say I was not here as your critic.

HUME: Oh. So you are not a friendly teacher after all.

SOCRATES: But I am. Is there any better proof of friendship—and of good teaching—than to subject all our ideas to critique? Is that not what you did?

Were you not the great opponent of dogmatic systems of all kinds?

HUME: I was indeed.

SOCRATES: Then you will not object to being subjected to the same kind of critique yourself.

HUME: I have no fear. I am not a dogmatic system builder, like those Rationalists Descartes and Spinoza and Leibniz.

SOCRATES: That remains to be seen.

HUME: Oh . . .

SOCRATES: Your face shows some fear, though you say you have none.

HUME: I do have some fear. I fear that you will play the part of Descartes, the dogmatic Rationalist, and I will play the part of Montaigne, the skeptic that Descartes tried to answer. You see, the three of us —you, Descartes, and myself—all were confronted with skeptics—you with the Sophists, Descartes with Montaigne, and myself with Pierre Bayle. But you and Descartes tried to refute your skeptics, whereas I learned from mine. So it seems we are on fundamentally different sides.

SOCRATES: If you don't mind my saying so, I am somewhat skeptical of your categories of skepticism versus dogmatism. I do not think we should begin by setting up these two sides, the skeptic and the dogmatist, and choosing sides at the beginning.

HUME: Why not?

SOCRATES: Because even if there are these two "sides", surely both "sides", if they are honest, have in common something more important than what separates them.

HUME: What is that? They seem to have nothing in common. They contradict each other. One side says we can know the truth with certainty, and the other side says we cannot.

SOCRATES: The common premise is that both sides honestly *seek* the truth.

HUME: Oh. But honest seeking is only the bare precondition for philosophizing.

SOCRATES: That precondition may be the most important thing of all. Tell me, do you feel more one with a dishonest skeptic or with an honest dogmatist?

HUME: Why do you ask that?

SOCRATES: Because if you are more one with the dishonest skeptic, then it is your ideological agreement about your skeptical conclusion that matters the most to you. And, if that is so, I think you are really a dogmatist. If, on the other hand, you are more one with the honest dogmatist, who is skeptical of skepticism, than with the dishonest believer in skepticism, then I think that you and I are at one on the very deepest level.

HUME: I think you are right, Socrates. But I am surprised to hear you say that.

SOCRATES: Why?

HUME: Because when you philosophized back in ancient Athens, if Plato's accounts are correct, you always put the reason above the will, but now you seem to be putting the will above the reason. You were not a voluntarist, but now you seem to be one: you seem to be presupposing the primacy of the will over the mind. For honesty is a choice of the will. It is the will to truth, the will to follow the argument wherever it goes. The choice to be honest and to *seek* the truth is made in the will, or the heart, while the claim to *find* the truth is made in the mind, or the head.

SOCRATES: Whether my own views on the relation between the mind and the will have changed since I lived on earth is not important now. We are not here to watch a contest between Hume and Socrates, but between Hume and Truth.

HUME: So your point is that even if you are a dogmatist and I am a skeptic, we are allied in honesty.

SOCRATES: Yes. But I do not say I am a dogmatist. Surely one can be neither a skeptic nor a dogmatist.

HUME: How? Either you claim certainty, like the dogmatics, or you do not, like the skeptics. Either there is or there is not certainty. Those are the only two options, logically. How can there be a third one? What escapes the either/or of dogmatism versus skepticism?

SOCRATES: Questioning!

HUME: What do you mean?

SOCRATES: I mean that skeptics do not question, once they have accepted skepticism, for they have despaired of finding the truth with certainty. And dogmatists do not question, because they think they already have the truth with certainty. True philosophers, it seems to me, are between these two. They are "lovers of

wisdom", and they question, because they believe that
wisdom exists and can be found, unlike the skeptics.
But they question also because they believe that they
do not yet have that wisdom yet, and there they are
unlike the dogmatists.

HUME: I am not that kind of simple and absolute skeptic, Socrates. I believe we can know truth. I just don't
think we can know it with certainty, only with probability. So I am a moderate or mitigated skeptic. I am
not a dogmatic skeptic.

SOCRATES: I see. So you do not claim to know that
you cannot know.

HUME: Of course not. That is a self-contradiction.

SOCRATES: So you are skeptical even about your skepticism.

HUME: Yes. I am open to questions at all times, about
anything, including questions about my skepticism. I
do not say it is true that there is no truth, or that I am
certain that no one is certain. I leave these questions
open for further investigation.

SOCRATES: Good. For that is why we are here: for
further investigation of these questions.

HUME: I put my arguments for skepticism in more
carefully considered words when I wrote my book,
and I will try to remember these arguments for you
now. Unless I can actually read my own words. I don't
suppose you have my book here?

SOCRATES: We do indeed. You will find a copy in your
hand, and another in mine.

HUME: Why, here it is indeed! This *must* be a dream. For otherwise, it is a miracle.

SOCRATES: Is *that* your famous argument against miracles? If so, it sounds very dogmatic rather than skeptical.

HUME: Of course not. I was just wondering where the books came from.

SOCRATES: They came from need and necessity. This is the place where you get whatever you need.

HUME: How does that happen?

SOCRATES: That happens simply because that is the nature of this place, just as rain happens to fall on thirsty plants to supply their need in the other world simply because that is the nature of that place.

HUME: Is it then indeed a miracle?

SOCRATES: That depends on how you define the term. It comes from what is natural to this world rather than from what is supernatural to it, so I would not call that a miracle here. Although it would surely be labeled a miracle on earth.

HUME: You know, of course, my skepticism of miracles.

SOCRATES: I know. And we will deal with your critique of miracles later. But, for now, it is enough that you understand that I am here as your rain, to supply your need. That is why I will subject your book to a critical questioning. It is my way of teaching, and teaching is to a mind what rain is to a plant.

HUME: I do not understand this new world, but I will accept my role in it—as long as neither you nor I but the argument is the master in our conversations. I am most willing to follow the lead of reason.

SOCRATES: Good! Then I invite you to climb aboard and see where the river of reason takes our boats.

2

The Point of Departure

HUME: Where shall we begin?

SOCRATES: Let me make a radical suggestion: that we begin at the beginning.

HUME: You are ironic, as usual.

SOCRATES: No, I am not. I mean it literally. "Radical" means "concerning roots", and that is why the most radical thing we could do would be to begin at the beginning. For if the root rots, the plant dies; and if you tear a plant up by its root, the whole plant is torn up. But if it is only a leaf or a flower that rots, or is torn off, the rest of the plant can still be healthy.

HUME: The point of your analogy is . . . ?

SOCRATES: That your philosophy depends only partially on any of its later, derivative leaves or branches, but totally on its roots, its first assumptions and starting points. So the most radical thing we can do is to find these and examine them.

HUME: I disagree. That is true only of deductive, rationalistic systems of philosophy, like Descartes' or Spinoza's or Leibniz'. All three tried to imitate the method of geometry. I am an Empiricist, not a Rationalist; and that means not only that I believe that all human knowledge begins with and depends on sense experience rather than on pure reason or "innate ideas", but also that my *method* will be empirical: I will reason from particulars known in sense experience, inductively, rather than from abstract general ideas, deductively.

SOCRATES: That is precisely one of the questions I want to investigate at the outset.

HUME: You mean whether we should philosophize by induction from experience rather than by deduction from general principles?

SOCRATES: No, whether *you do.*

HUME: Of course I do. As I told you, I am an Empiricist, not a Rationalist.

SOCRATES: And I am Socrates, and I have this bothersome habit of questioning everything, including your claim about yourself. That favorite maxim of mine, "know thyself"—if we all did that easily and automatically, and infallibly, we wouldn't need to inquire, would we?

HUME: I suppose not. Inquire away, then.

SOCRATES: I am inquiring about two things: your starting point and your method. Are they both empirical, as you claim?

HUME: I see you opening my book. I should explain that you will not find my starting point in Section I, which is just an introduction, an explanation of the kind of philosophy I intend to do. You will find it instead at the beginning of Section II, where I say that the origin of all our ideas is experience, that all our ideas are derived from sense impressions. That is my Empiricism.

SOCRATES: Yes it is. And from that starting point you derive many conclusions—skeptical conclusions about abstract ideas, and about causality, and about certainty, and later about miracles and about many other things, such as free will, and life after death, and the compatibility between faith and reason.

HUME: Indeed I do.

SOCRATES: But that process, by which you derive these conclusions—is that not deduction?

HUME: Oh, of course.

SOCRATES: Then your *method* is just as rationalistic as that of Descartes and the rationalists; it is only your *starting point* point that is different.

HUME: No, for my starting point changes everything, including my method. I do not claim to deduce new truths with certainty, as the Rationalists do. I only *arrange* my thoughts deductively, but I do not *derive* them deductively. I derive them inductively, from experience. An Empiricist does not reject deductive reasoning; he just puts it in its place, as a servant of experience rather than its lord. As Hobbes said, Reason is "the scout for the senses".

SOCRATES: I understand.

HUME: I think perhaps you *don't* understand, Socrates. Please let me explain what I intend to do before you examine my doing it. That's why I put

Section I first. If you really want to begin at my beginning, that is where you should begin, rather than jumping immediately to Section II, where I state my Empiricist premise about the origin of all our ideas.

SOCRATES: That is the premise from which you derive your conclusions, is it not?

HUME: It is.

SOCRATES: So we should begin there, should we not?

HUME: You say that because you are a Rationalist; you are so rationalistic that all you care about is the deductive logical system. I know your method, Socrates. You will examine my premise, defining its terms and asking whether it is true and if so, *why* it is true, and then you will investigate whether my answer to *that* question (the question about why is the premise for my premise is true) is not my *real* first premise. And then you will investigate whether all my conclusions follow with logical necessity from my premises. That is exactly what a Rationalist would worry about: defining terms, proving premises, and examining the logic of arguments. But I am not a Rationalist, so that is not my primary concern.

SOCRATES: What is logic to you, then?

HUME: Logic to me is simply the way I arrange the coins of my thoughts. Two more important questions are where these thoughts in fact come from, and, second, where they go to in my hands, that is, what I want to do with them, for what purpose I am considering them and using them.

SOCRATES: So that is why you want to begin with your introduction: because *those* questions are dealt with there.

HUME: Exactly. You see, I fear that you will misinterpret the whole point of my philosophy if you do not understand my intentions for it.

SOCRATES: I accept your correction. Let us defer the question of your Empiricist premise, then, and begin with your introduction, your first section.

HUME: Thank you.

SOCRATES: Here is what seems to me to be the gist of what you say in Section I. It is about the relation between philosophy and life.

E, I   **Moral philosophy, the science of human nature, may be treated after two different manners . . . one considers man chiefly as born for action; and as influenced . . . by taste and sentiment, pursuing one object, and avoiding another, according to the value which these objects seem to possess. . . . This species of philosophers . . . please the imagination and engage the affections. . . .**

The other species of philosophers considers man in the light of a reasonable rather than an active being, and endeavours to form his understanding more than cultivate his manners. They regard human nature as a subject of speculation, and . . . examine it, in order to find those principles, which regulate our understanding.

You say, then, that *speculative* philosophy is only a small part of human life, and most of life is concerned with the more practical matters of our desires, affections, and feelings rather than abstract thought, general principles, or scientific explanations. Is that a fair summary of your point?

HUME: Yes.

SOCRATES: And you contrast not only these two different kinds of thinking, but also the two different kinds of people who pursue these two different kinds of thinking, when you say that

> **The mere philosopher is a character . . . little**   E, I
> **acceptable in the world, as being supposed to**
> **contribute nothing either to the advantage**
> **or pleasure of society; while he lives remote**
> **from communication with mankind, and is**
> **wrapped up in principles and notions equally**
> **remote from their comprehension.**

And then your advice to the philosopher is to despise neither ordinary life nor speculative philosophy, but to embrace both. You say: **"Be a philosopher; but amidst all your philosophy, be still a man."**

HUME: I rather like that line, Socrates. Would you not call it a piece of wisdom?

SOCRATES: I would indeed.

HUME: So what do you question now?

SOCRATES: Whether you lived this wisdom, whether you practiced what you preached.

HUME: I neglected neither the constraints of philosophy nor the pleasures of ordinary life.

SOCRATES: But did you ever connect them? Did your philosophy inform your life? Did you not complain of the stark disconnect between these two when you wrote, in Book I of your longer work, the *Treatise on Human Nature*,[1]

THN I, IV, §7

But before I launch out into those immense depths of philosophy, which lie before me, I find myself inclined to stop a moment in my present station, and to ponder that voyage, which I have undertaken. . . .

I am first affrighted and confounded with that forelorn solitude, in which I am placed in my philosophy, and fancy myself some strange uncouth monster, who not being able to mingle and unite in society, has been expelled all human commerce, and left utterly abandoned and disconsolate.

You write of your need to leave your philosophical work and play backgammon or checkers in order to regain a footing in the real world. If your philosophy did not give you that footing, what good is it? And how empirical, how true to experience can it be? Is it not as far removed from the daily experience of life in this world as any rationalistic system is? Is it not like Laputa, the philosophers' island in the sky in Swift's *Gulliver's Travels*?

---

[1] Texts quoted from Hume's *Treatise on Human Nature* are indicated as THN in the sidenotes.

HUME: I *did* practice what I preached. I wrote: **"Be a philosopher; but . . . be still a man."** I did not write:

"Be sure you connect the two happily." I thought you were here to investigate my thoughts, not my life, Socrates.

SOCRATES: That is true.

HUME: What fault do you find with my thought?

SOCRATES: The same fault you yourself admitted you found with your life: a lack of integration between your thought and your life.

HUME: That is the fault of my life, which you said you were not here to examine.

SOCRATES: But I think it may be the fault of your thought, which I *am* here to examine. Perhaps your thought is not livable.

HUME: What right do you have to come to that judgmental conclusion?

SOCRATES: The right of one who reads your books. For you yourself admit this judgment, in so many words. We shall examine some of those words shortly.

HUME: If I cannot live my philosophy, that is the fault of my life, not of my philosophy.

SOCRATES: Not if you are an Empiricist, as you make yourself out to be.

HUME: Why do you say that?

SOCRATES: Because of your own definition of the Rationalism you reject and the Empiricism you embrace. Tell me, is this not the fundamental distinction between these two philosophies, that the Rationalist believes in abstract principles that he has not derived from experience or tested by experience, and when experience seems to contradict them, he forces experience to conform to his theory rather than altering the theory to conform to his experience—is that not what you mean by a Rationalist?

HUME: It is indeed. Surely you are not suggesting that I am guilty of the very philosophical sin I reject so strongly and famously?

SOCRATES: We shall see. And then would not the opposite kind of philosopher from the Rationalist be the Empiricist?

HUME: Yes.

SOCRATES: And would not the Empiricist be one who tailors his philosophy to his experience rather than vice versa?

HUME: Yes . . .

SOCRATES: And is your life, as it is actually lived, part of your experience or part of your system of rational principles?

HUME: Part of my experience, of course.

SOCRATES: Then if you tailor your philosophy to your experience, you must tailor your philosophy to your life, to your lived experience.

HUME: Of course.

SOCRATES: But you said that your life told you that your philosophy was unlivable, that it prevented you from being a man as well as a philosopher.

HUME: I did admit that.

SOCRATES: So why did you not alter your philosophical theories to fit your experience? Why did you not learn from your experience? Why did you not let your experience judge and test and refute your philosophy? Would not that have been the Empiricist thing to do? On the contrary, you maintained your theories in the teeth of experience. Is that not a Rationalist thing to do?

HUME: So you accuse me of being a Rationalist!

SOCRATES: The definition seems to fit. And here is another definition of Rationalism that seems to fit. Rationalism, as put forth in Descartes and Spinoza, insists on clear and distinct ideas . . .

HUME: That is true . . .

SOCRATES: But in experience, things are usually mixed, not pure.

HUME: Much of the time, yes. Where do you say I insist on clear and distinct ideas like a Rationalist?

SOCRATES: Here at the very beginning of your book, in the distinction you draw between philosophy and life. These are so different to you that they look like two of Descartes' "clear and distinct ideas", like his famous distinction between the mind and the body, a dividing line that he drew with such absolute clarity that it made humanity fall off the wall and split into two pieces like Humpty Dumpty, and ever since

Descartes, "all the king's horses and all the king's men couldn't put Humpty Dumpty back together again." Your division between philosophy and life seems to be very much like Descartes' division between mind and body: it is sharp and clear, and it is rationalistic rather than experiential. Hardly any other philosopher ever had such a disconnect between his philosophy and his life. Experience and history have shown many examples of the happy mingling of philosophy and life. I modestly put myself forward as Exhibit A of this happy mingling.

HUME: So you are faulting me for . . . what, exactly? For not being as *happy* as you?

SOCRATES: No, I am faulting you because your philosophy was not empirical enough. I am faulting you for being a Rationalist in Empiricist's clothing.

HUME: You have not proved this, you have only stated it.

SOCRATES: That is true. It is only my suspicion, and I have not proved my suspicion yet. What I am doing now is only introducing myself and what I intend to show you in this examination, just as in Section I you introduce yourself and what you intend to show in your book.

HUME: So this is not your judgment but your suspicion—not your conclusion at the end of your investigation but your impression at the beginning.

SOCRATES: Yes.

HUME: Then since you do not yet claim to judge my philosophy, I will not claim to judge your judgment.

We are both only beginning our investigation, not ending it.

SOCRATES: I thank you for being so reasonable. But I must share one other reason for my suspicion that you are a Rationalist, which comes from the other major point in the first section of your book.

HUME: What is that?

SOCRATES: It is where you tell us what you hope to accomplish with your philosophy:

> **But may we not hope, that philosophy, if**   E, I
> **cultivated with care . . . may . . . discover,**
> **at least in some degree, the secret springs**
> **and principles, by which the human mind**
> **is actuated in its operations? Astronomers**
> **had long contented themselves with prov-**
> **ing, from the phaenomena, the true motions,**
> **order, and magnitude of the heavenly bod-**
> **ies. Till a philosopher at last arose [New-**
> **ton] who seems, from the happiest reason-**
> **ing, to have also determined the laws and**
> **forces, by which the revolutions of the plan-**
> **ets are governed and directed. The like has**
> **been performed with regard to other parts**
> **of nature. And there is no reason to despair**
> **of equal success in our enquiries concern-**
> **ing the mental powers and economy, if pros-**
> **ecuted with equal capacity and caution.**

Here you make an analogy with Newton in explaining what your science of ideas intends to accomplish: as Newton reduced the complex phenomena of the behavior of all matter to a few explanatory principles, you reduce the complex phenomena of the behavior of all consciousness to a few explanatory principles. And that too seems more like a Rationalist ideal than the Empiricist one.

HUME: The analogy with Newton is apt, I believe. He discovered the three laws of motion, including gravity, which govern the motion of matter. Gravity is a physical connection of association between particles of matter. And I discovered the three laws of association that govern the motion of thought, the laws of gravity between particles of thought, so to speak: a kind of mental gravity. I summarize these in Section III:

E, III   **Though it be too obvious to escape observation, that different ideas are connected together; I do not find that any philosopher has attempted to enumerate or class all the principles of association; a subject, however, that seems worthy of curiosity. To me, there appear to be only three principles of connexion among ideas, namely, *Resemblance, Contiguity* in time or place, and *Cause* or *Effect*.**

That these principles serve to connect ideas will not, I believe, be much doubted. A picture naturally leads our thoughts to the original: [This is an example of Resemblance.] **The mention of one apartment in a building naturally introduces an enquiry or discourse concerning the others:** [This is an example of Contiguity.] **and if we think of a wound, we can scarcely forbear reflecting on the pain which follows it.** [This is an example of Cause or Effect.]

SOCRATES: This is why I suspect you of Rationalism, you see. I know you reject innate ideas and trace all ideas to sense impressions in your epistemology. That is your theory. But your practice in doing philosophy seems highly rationalistic: not only is it a deductive system but it is a simplistic, reductionistic one: the complexity of experience is reduced to a few simple abstract principles.

HUME: What you call reductionism is simply the goal of all science, Socrates. Science always seeks to explain the complex by the simple, the phenomena by the hypothesis, and the best hypothesis is expressed in a formula.

SOCRATES: I grant that. But that is not pure Empiricism.

HUME: Labels do not matter. Science remains science, whether it is called Empiricist or Rationalist.

SOCRATES: Fine, but there is another aspect of your Rationalism. It is your reductionism.

HUME: What do you mean by "reductionism"?

SOCRATES: I mean your penchant for claiming that A is *nothing but* B. I might call this your "nothing buttery." The upshot of each point in your philosophy is to dispute ordinary thought, or common sense.

HUME: You did that too, Socrates, don't you remember?

SOCRATES: Ah, but you dispute it not for being too small, like a cave, but too big, like a fantasy. If you were Hamlet, you would not say to Horatio that "there are more things in heaven and earth than are dreamed of in your philosophy." You would say there is *less*.

HUME: I cannot help coming to conclusions that are more skeptical than common sense. Common sense is naïve and credulous.

SOCRATES: But I mean by "reductionism" not only your skeptical *conclusions* but above all your *method*.

HUME: What do you fault about my method?

SOCRATES: As I said, it seems highly rationalistic.

HUME: And as *I* said, I am the enemy of the Rationalists!

SOCRATES: As an epistemological theory, yes, but not as a method. Your method, like theirs, is to reduce the data to the explanation, the complex to the simple, the rich variety of experience to simple universal formulas.

HUME: But that is simply one of the features of the scientific method.

SOCRATES: Does that mean it should be one of the features of the philosophical method?

HUME: There is nothing absolutely true or false about a method, Socrates. A method is simply a tool, a practical means to the end of finding the truth. What we should argue about is the truth.

SOCRATES: I agree. But might it not be *true* that the scientific method is no more fitting for the philosopher than a nonscientific method is for a scientist?

HUME: And what method would you use to compare the scientific method with any other method?

SOCRATES: I would use the universal method of logic.

HUME: Fair enough.

SOCRATES: And I say that reductionism violates the laws of logic.

HUME: How?

SOCRATES: Because the formula for all reductionism is that "S is nothing but P", is this not true?

HUME: Yes.

SOCRATES: And does this not mean that there is nothing more in S than P, that there is no "S-that-is-more-than-P"?

HUME: It does. What is the problem with that?

SOCRATES: The problem is that that claims to know that there is no "S-that-is-more-than-P", does it not?

HUME: It does. I still don't see the problem.

SOCRATES: The problem is that that claims to know that there is *in all reality* no "S-that-is-more-than-P".

HUME: Yes. I still don't see . . .

SOCRATES: And *that* claim presupposes the knowledge of all reality.

HUME: Oh.

SOCRATES: Which is a claim only omniscience can make.

HUME: So you are saying that reductionism logically claims omniscience?

SOCRATES: Exactly. And that is precisely the arrogant dogmatism that you set out to destroy, the dragon you set out to slay. Are you sure you are not yourself a dragon?

HUME: What an absurd accusation!

SOCRATES: So you are not a Rationalist dragon?

HUME: Indeed not.

SOCRATES: Are you sure?

HUME: I am.

SOCRATES: And I am *not* sure. Which of us is now the skeptic and which of us the Rationalist, claiming certainty?

HUME: I do not claim certainty. If my words seemed to claim that, I retract them.

SOCRATES: You are not certain, then, that certainty is impossible?

HUME: That is an old and well-known dilemma loved by Rationalists. If I say I am *certain* of *this*, then I am not a skeptic. But if I say I am *not* certain that we cannot attain certainty, then I open the door to claims to certainty, to Rationalism.

SOCRATES: And how do you answer this dilemma?

HUME: It is an unfair dilemma. If this dilemma is valid, no one can be a skeptic. But I am a skeptic. But mine is not the absolute skepticism that the dilemma reveals as self-contradictory, but a moderate or mitigated skepticism.

SOCRATES: And do you have moderate skepticism about this moderate skepticism of yours?

HUME: I do indeed, without self-contradiction.

SOCRATES: Then you are open to correction.

HUME: I am.

SOCRATES: Then we can proceed with good hope of learning something new. I think it is now time to investigate your starting point and assumption. But I think we should explore your historical starting point first, before we explore your logical starting point.

HUME: What do you mean by that?

SOCRATES: That we should look at where *you* began before we look at where your *arguments* begin. That we should look at the philosopher that influenced you the most historically, before we concentrate on your philosophy alone and ask where it begins logically.

HUME: That philosopher would be John Locke, I suppose. But why do you want to explore my relation to Locke before exploring my book? I thought we were here to explore my book.

SOCRATES: Because we can understand your book better if we place it in that historical context. We should know what went on in "the great conversation" just before you entered it.

HUME: Fine. Let us do so.

3

Hume's Relation to Locke

SOCRATES: Like you, John Locke wrote about the origin of ideas.

HUME: That is one way I follow in his footsteps.

SOCRATES: And like you, Locke believed that all ideas originated in sense experience.

HUME: And that is another way I follow him. We are both classified as Empiricists.

SOCRATES: Did you agree with Locke's epistemology and simply draw more radical consequences from it?

HUME: Not entirely. I agreed with Locke on many things, but on a few things I disagreed. Is there any one of his ideas in particular that you want to ask me about?

SOCRATES: Yes: his idea of ideas. I mean his notion of what an idea is, what the word "idea" means. I wonder whether you mean the same thing he meant.

HUME: Why do you focus on that question?

SOCRATES: Because that is the starting point of his philosophy, and perhaps also of yours.

HUME: Then let us look at that starting point.

SOCRATES: Locke's very first proposition, in his *Essay Concerning Human Understanding*, is that "I mean by 'idea' 'object of thought'."

HUME: Why do you think that sentence is important? It seems quite noncontroversial.

SOCRATES: Because it contains two notions that *are* controversial. First, that the immediate objects of our consciousness, the first things we are aware of, are our own ideas, not the real things in the world that those ideas are ideas *of*.

And second, that these ideas in our minds (or our senses or our imaginations) are *copies*, or pictures, or representations, of real things outside our minds (or outside our senses or our imaginations). Do you accept these two notions too, as you seem to?

HUME: Why do you think I seem to accept them?

SOCRATES: Because you too, like Locke, begin by thinking about ideas, not about real things, so it seems that you too believe that we are first aware of ideas, and only then, after that, of the things these ideas tell us about. And if this is so, if you believe Locke's first notion, then you probably also believe his second notion, that these ideas tell us about real things by being copies or pictures or representations or images of these real things. And that seems like a commonly believed notion. I suppose that most people think of ideas as copies of things, as Locke does—something like pictures of the world taken by the mind's camera.

HUME: And why is it important to you whether this is my definition of "idea" as well as Locke's?

SOCRATES: Because if it is, I think your entire philosophy is mistaken insofar as it depends on this definition. For I am quite sure it is a very bad one.

HUME: Why?

SOCRATES: Because if it is true, if ideas are like pictures or copies of things, and if what we know directly and in the first place is only ideas, then we can never know which of these ideas are true copies of real things and which are not. If you never saw the real me, but only saw different pictures or statues of me, and these pictures were not the same, how could you know which pictures were true and which were false?

HUME: I suppose I couldn't.

SOCRATES: Do you understand why?

HUME: I think so. But please tell me how *you* understand it. Why do you think this skeptical conclusion follows from Locke's premises?

SOCRATES: It seems quite simple, really. But let us do this together. Tell me, what is the standard for judging the truth or falsity of any picture or image or copy?

HUME: The standard for judging an image of a real thing is the thing itself, of course: the thing the image is an image *of*.

SOCRATES: Indeed. And can we judge without knowing the standard of judgment?

HUME: No.

SOCRATES: So we cannot judge images if we do not know realities. Now tell me, what is the name for the philosophy that claims we cannot know realities, that we cannot judge what is really true and really false?

HUME: Skepticism.

SOCRATES: So Locke's premise leads to skepticism. For if we accept this premise of Locke's, we must believe that we are like prisoners in a cave seeing only shadows, or prisoners in a jail cell without windows, viewing only images of the outside world on a screen. The images may be true or they may be false, but unless we can look out the window and see the real tree, we cannot judge whether the image of the tree that we see on the screen is a faithful image or a distorted one. If we cannot know what the real weather is today, we can't tell whether the weather reports are true or not. And so if all we know directly are ideas, and if ideas are only images—in other words, if Locke's two premises are true—then we must end in skepticism, if we are logical, even though Locke did not.

HUME: You know that the conclusion of skepticism does not frighten me. A form of skepticism is my conclusion also, though it is not an absolute skepticism. But I have a surer road to that conclusion than Locke's road. I do *not* accept Locke's "copy theory" of ideas. In my earlier work I did assume that, but in this book I do not.

SOCRATES: Do you say, then, that we can know real things as they really are, and not just ideas? Do you disagree with Locke's first premise? Do you say that ideas are the *means by which* we can know real things, rather than *that which* we know?

HUME: I do not say either. I do not need to assume either. You are flogging a dead horse, Socrates. You are refuting a straw man. Hume is not Locke. Hume does not begin by defining "idea" as "object of knowledge". He begins by asking where we get our ideas.

SOCRATES: I see. But you do accept Locke's Empiricism, do you not?—that all ideas originate in sense experience?

HUME: I do. But so did the medieval Scholastic philosophers, like Thomas Aquinas, following Aristotle. One of their maxims was that "there is nothing in the intellect that was not first in the senses." That is a reasonable and traditional assumption. Only Descartes and his Rationalist disciples disagree with that.

SOCRATES: Are you sure?

HUME: Why? Who else but a Rationalist disagrees with that maxim?

SOCRATES: I think *you* do too.

HUME: What? Why?

SOCRATES: Because that maxim presupposes that there is such a thing as the intellect, and that it is not the same as the senses, and I think you do not believe that. But let us see whether you do or not. Would you not agree that the senses are physical, palpable?

HUME: Yes.

SOCRATES: But is the intellect physical and palpable? Can you see it, as you can see the eyes or ears?

HUME: No.

SOCRATES: So the senses are material and the intellect is not.

HUME: Yes.

SOCRATES: What is the word for "not material"?

HUME: "Immaterial".

SOCRATES: So the intellect is immaterial.

HUME: Yes, according to those who believe that such a thing exists.

SOCRATES: And you do not?

HUME: No.

SOCRATES: Then you do not agree with that medieval maxim, which presupposes that there *is* an immaterial intellect that is distinct from the material senses.

HUME: I do not. I do not accept ghosts or spirits, either inside or outside.

SOCRATES: What do you mean by "inside or outside"?

HUME: I do not accept the notion that there is a spirit or ghost in us called the intellect, and I do not believe that there are ghosts or spirits in the world outside us either. I call both ideas ancient superstitions. The intellect is simply the brain's power to think. It is material, not spiritual.

SOCRATES: I thought you thought that. So you are a materialist. But let's be sure. Let's look at another difference between the intellect and the senses. The senses perceive things in the world, do they not?

HUME: Yes.

SOCRATES: Do they perceive themselves? Are they reflexive, or self-conscious?

HUME: No. The eye can only see its reflection in a mirror.

SOCRATES: But we can think about ourselves, can't we?

HUME: Of course.

SOCRATES: Then the power or instrument with which we do that must be different than the senses. For we know ourselves, but the senses cannot know themselves.

HUME: That follows.

SOCRATES: This power of self-knowledge most people call the intellect. But you do not believe there *is* an intellect distinct from the senses, do you?

HUME: No. I do not accept the inner ghost, or soul, or substantial self.

SOCRATES: Either in yourself or in me?

HUME: In no one.

SOCRATES: If I am not a self, what am I?

HUME: You are nothing more than the sum total of all your sensations and the ideas that are copied from them.

SOCRATES: So there is no "self" to know?

HUME: No.

SOCRATES: So we cannot know ourselves.

HUME: No. Your famous puzzle was unsolvable, Socrates.

SOCRATES: Let us run a third test to be sure that you really reject the existence of an immaterial spirit or self or mind or intellect. Would you say that a third difference between the senses and the intellect is that the senses cannot have any abstract ideas, while the intellect can?

HUME: Yes, if there were such a thing as an intellect. For the senses cannot abstract treeness from trees, or justice from just acts.

SOCRATES: So only the intellect has abstract concepts, while the senses have only concrete percepts.

HUME: Yes. And I also deny abstract ideas. I am a Nominalist. I deny the existence of universal concepts. As I wrote:

> **Let any man try to conceive a triangle in general, which is neither *Isosceles* nor *Scalenum*, nor has any particular length or proportion of sides; and he will soon perceive the absurdity of all the scholastic notions with regard to abstraction and general ideas.**

E, XII

SOCRATES: So you say that every thing in the world is particular, not general, and also that every idea in the mind is particular, not general.

HUME: Yes.

SOCRATES: And particular things are different from each other? You and I, for instance?

HUME: Yes.

SOCRATES: But a universal would not be different. For instance, if there were such a thing as universal human nature, it would be the same in the two of us.

HUME: Yes. But there is no such thing. There are only different individual things, and not any one sameness in all of them. All things are different.

SOCRATES: Do you not see the logical self-contradiction in saying that?

HUME: What self-contradiction?

SOCRATES: If all things are different, how can we call them all "things"?

HUME: Universals are only words. That is the meaning of "Nominalism". We use common nouns as a kind of shorthand, instead of referring to each thing by a proper name, as we refer to each human being by a proper name.

SOCRATES: But how can you classify them all as "human beings"? In the very act of stating Nominalism, you refute it.

HUME: We apply the same name to two or more individual things that are the same in some way but different in other ways. We distinguish constants from variables.

SOCRATES: Can we distinguish constants from variables without apprehending variables?

HUME: Of course not.

SOCRATES: And can we distinguish constants from variables without apprehending constants?

HUME: Of course not.

SOCRATES: And we do distinguish constants from variables?

HUME: Yes.

SOCRATES: Then we do apprehend constants.

HUME: Yes.

SOCRATES: And that is apprehending what is common or general to two or more particulars.

HUME: Yes.

SOCRATES: And if this apprehension is true, it must be true of real things.

HUME: Yes.

SOCRATES: Then these constants, or common features, must be real.

HUME: Yes.

SOCRATES: But to say they are *common* is to say they are *universal*.

HUME: The two words do seem to mean the same thing.

SOCRATES: So universals are real after all. But you said you were a Nominalist. Nominalism denies that universals are real.

HUME: I deny Platonic Ideas. There are only two men here, Hume and Socrates. There are not three men, Hume and Socrates and Universal Humanity, or Human Nature.

SOCRATES: Oh, but that is surely a "straw man". You do not need to go as far as Plato went to believe in universals and overcome Nominalism. You do not need to say that these universals exist separate from individual things, as Plato did. You need only say that universals exist *in* individual things, as Aristotle did. So you do not need to say that there are three men here, Socrates and Hume and Humanity, only two; but you do need to say that both of the two of us share, or participate in, the same essential nature of being human. In fact, the argument you used, the "third man" argument, was Aristotle's argument against Plato.

HUME: I do not want to admit even that kind of objective reality for universal natures. For the ideas by which we apprehend universal natures are abstract ideas, and I deny abstract ideas.

SOCRATES: But surely you can know that the two of us are human beings and that our clothes and books are not human beings? Do you admit that you can know that much?

HUME: Yes.

SOCRATES: But you need universals to do that.

HUME: I don't need universals.

SOCRATES: Can you apprehend me as a particular man?

HUME: Indeed I can. You are a particular, not a universal. So I can apprehend you.

SOCRATES: So you can apprehend me not just as a particular but as a particular *man*?

HUME: Yes.

SOCRATES: But to apprehend me as a particular *man* —is this not to apprehend me as an instance of a certain kind or nature or species—man, not bird?

HUME: Yes.

SOCRATES: And does that not involve an understanding of that species or kind or nature?

HUME: That does seem to be a problem. But if I am an Empiricist, I must be a Nominalist. For the senses, as you yourself admit, know no universals. But I would prefer not to get into the abstract Scholastic arguments about universals here. I thought we were here to examine my book.

SOCRATES: We are. But your Nominalism is a hidden presupposition of your Empiricism, so it is fair game. And so are the *consequences* of Empiricism.

HUME: What consequences?

SOCRATES: The most radical one is this: that man, the rational animal, differs from the irrational animals only in degree, not in kind or essence or species. If we do not have intellects distinct from the senses, as the animals do not, if we only have imaginations, like animals, then we are only like animals.

HUME: That is indeed my conclusion.

SOCRATES: A radical one indeed. And one that can easily be refuted, I think. For we can obviously conceive as well as imagine. Our understanding transcends our imagination.

HUME: Prove it.

SOCRATES: Can you understand a square and a triangle?

HUME: Of course.

SOCRATES: Can you imagine them?

HUME: Yes.

SOCRATES: Can you understand the difference between them?

HUME: Yes. But only because I can imagine it.

SOCRATES: Can you understand the difference between a 103-sided figure and a 104-sided figure?

HUME: Yes. I can do geometry.

SOCRATES: Can you imagine the difference?

HUME: I must be able to, if I can understand it.

SOCRATES: Can you imagine a 103-sided figure?

HUME: No.

SOCRATES: Can you imagine a 104-sided figure?

HUME: No.

SOCRATES: Then how can you imagine the difference between them?

HUME: I suppose I can't.

SOCRATES: Then you can understand something that you cannot imagine.

HUME: I thought we were going to explore my book rather than these abstract arguments about Nominalism and Empiricism in general.

SOCRATES: Two general ideas. See? We do have general ideas.

HUME: Not clear ones. As I write in the next chapter,

> **All ideas, especially abstract ones, are naturally faint and obscure: the mind has but a slender hold of them: they are apt to be confounded with other resembling ideas.**
>
> **On the contrary, all impressions, that is, all sensations, either outward or inward, are strong and vivid: the limits between them are more exactly determined: nor is it easy to fall into any error or mistake with regard to them.**

E, II, 3

SOCRATES: But surely the idea of two, or the idea of triangle, or the idea of the essence of humanity as soul and body, rational animal, is clearer and more distinct than the twoness of Adam and Eve, or the triangularity of the Great Pyramid, or the humanness of Neanderthals. It is the world of the senses that appears as a "buzzing, blooming confusion" while the world of abstract ideas is more clear and distinct. Geometry is clearer than surveying, and anatomy is clearer than your body. And it is easier to make mistakes in surveying than to make mistakes in geometry, easier to make mistakes about your body than to make mistakes on an anatomy examination.

HUME: No, Socrates, I say it is the opposite. But to explain why requires us to go deeper into my book.

SOCRATES: Then let us do just that.

4

Hume's Premise:
The Origin of All Ideas

SOCRATES: After your introduction, in Section I, which was *about* philosophy, the first claim *in* your philosophy is the very beginning of Section II, which you entitle "Of the Origin of Ideas".

HUME: That is indeed my starting point, and it is pure Empiricism.

SOCRATES: Whatever label fits it, here it is:

E, II   **Everyone will readily allow, that there is a considerable difference between the perceptions of the mind, when a man feels the pain of excessive heat, or the pleasure of moderate warmth, and when he afterwards recalls to his memory this sensation, or anticipates it by his imagination. These faculties may mimic or copy the perceptions of the senses; but they never can entirely reach the force and vivacity of the original sentiment.**

I think I understand the distinction you make here, but your terminology is unusual. When you speak of "the perceptions of the *mind*" such as pain, heat, and pleasure, you seem to mean the direct experience of the *senses,* for you later call this "sensation" and "sentiment". When you contrast these with "memory and imagination", you seem to be referring to something more mental and less physical, something more like a concept or idea rather than a direct sense perception. Is that correct?

HUME: Yes. On the same page I call these two things "impressions" and "ideas", respectively:

> **Here therefore we may divide all the percep-** E, II
> **tions of the mind into two classes or species,**
> **which are distinguished by their different de-**
> **grees of force and vivacity. The less forcible**
> **and lively are commonly denominated *Thoughts***
> **or *Ideas*. The other species . . . let us . . . call**
> **them *Impressions* . . . By the term *impression*,**
> **then, I mean all our more lively perceptions,**
> **when we hear, or see, or feel, or love, or hate,**
> **or desire, or will.**

SOCRATES: So in the first paragraph you use "perceptions of the mind" to mean impressions, as distinct from ideas, and in the second paragraph you use the same term, "the perceptions of the mind", to mean both impressions *and* ideas. For you divide the genus "the perceptions of the mind" into those two species.

HUME: Yes. I used the term loosely. But I trust my point is clear.

SOCRATES: Not to me, alas. For when you gave the two examples of "the pain of excessive heat" and "the pleasure of moderate warmth" in your first paragraph, I thought you meant by "impressions" only "*sensory* impressions", or sensations. But in your second paragraph you give seven examples of "impressions", and only the first three are sensations: "hear, or see, or feel". These are three of the five senses. But your other four examples cannot be performed with any of the five senses: "love, or hate, or desire, or will". So I am still unclear about your categories.

HUME: My distinction between "impressions" and "ideas" is not the same as the distinction between "sensations" and "concepts". Impressions are the immediate, lively acts of the mind, or awareness, or consciousness, whether sensory or emotional or volitional. Ideas are the pale copies of impressions, whether in the senses or the emotions or the will.

SOCRATES: You speak of senses, emotions, and will. What about the intellect?

HUME: That too. But I deny that there are any intellectual impressions, only intellectual ideas. The intellect is always in the "less lively" category.

SOCRATES: What an unusual thing for an intellectual like yourself to say!
    I also do not understand how your four nonsensory examples of impressions—love, hate, desire, and will—are four. They seem to be only three, at the most. For what most people mean by "love" comes under either "desire", such as my love for food, or sex, or beauty, or truth—the Greek word for that is *eros*—or else it comes under "will", which is the case with charity, the deliberate choice to will and seek the good of another person. (The Greek word for that is *agape*.)

But these are only problems with inexact terminology. Your main point is clear: the distinction between sense impressions and ideas.

HUME: Thank you for not quibbling over the terminology.

SOCRATES: On the other hand, your main point is *not* clear, now that I think of it again. For you say that the difference between ideas and impressions is a matter of degree, "degree of force or vivacity".

HUME: What is unclear about that?

SOCRATES: I wonder, first, what kind of "force" is this? Simply the mental force of vividness?

HUME: Yes.

SOCRATES: But how can one perception be more "lively" than another? Do you mean "clearer", or "more memorable", or "more attended with strong emotion", or "more unable to be ignored", or "more surprising" or "new" or "unpredictable", or what?

And if the only difference between ideas and impressions is a matter of degree (for you say that impressions are "more" lively), then the difference between ideas and impressions is only conventional, and relative, like the difference between "stupid" and "smart", which may be set at any intelligence level, or like the difference between child and adult, which may be set by convention at any age. In that case, there are not two species in reality, but only in your conventional categorizing of the single continuum of more or less.

HUME: No, Socrates, they are two species.

SOCRATES: Even though their difference in vivacity is only relative?

HUME: Yes, since the difference in vivacity is not their specific difference.

SOCRATES: I think you can guess what my next question will be, then.

HUME: What *is* their specific difference? Well, to begin with, I do not like to speak of any "specific differences" at all, because that is the Scholastic language of metaphysics, rather than the language of Nominalism. It seems to presuppose the existence of real species, real universals. But I will use the conventional language for your sake, though I repudiate its metaphysical baggage. If I can use "specific difference" to mean simply "that which clearly distinguishes two things, and which is more than a matter of relative degree", then the specific difference between impressions and ideas is that impressions are immediate, while ideas are not. Ideas are later, and *derived* from impressions. They are *copies* of impressions. An original painting and a copy may be very similar to each other in many ways and may differ only in degree of vivacity; yet the original is not at all a copy, and the copy is not at all an original. So there is a specific difference, and it is in their relationship to each other, the relationship of copy versus original. Ideas are copies of impressions.

SOCRATES: I see. Thank you. You have made that point clear now. Locke said that all our ideas and impressions were also copies of real things. Do you say the same, or not?

HUME: I don't think we need to begin by either agreeing or disagreeing with Locke's definition. I begin *not* with the relation between ideas (in Locke's broad sense of the word, including what I call both "impressions" and "ideas") and real things—that was the issue that caused us such trouble in our last conversation—but instead with the relation between "ideas" (in my narrower sense of "ideas") and "impressions". I begin with the architecture of the mind, not with the architecture of the world—with epistemology, not metaphysics.

SOCRATES: So you begin within the mind, not with the relation between the mind and the world.

HUME: Yes. But the fact that I begin within the mind does not mean that I claim that we know our own minds first, before we know the world. That was Descartes' claim: that our first certain knowledge was "I think therefore I am." I do not believe that. If I did, I would be a Rationalist.

SOCRATES: But you too see "ideas" (in your narrower sense, the sense in which they are contrasted with "impressions") as copies: copies of impressions, rather than copies of things.

HUME: Yes.

SOCRATES: And are the impressions copies of things?

HUME: I will not say that. I implied that in my first, longer book, and I deliberately avoided saying that in this later, shorter book, for I will not be trapped into your refutation of Locke. If you wish, let us say that impressions are not copies of things, but the direct knowing of things.

SOCRATES: Fine—though that admission would seem to compromise your skepticism.

HUME: Call it semi-skepticism if you wish. Let us not argue about labels.

SOCRATES: Agreed. So I think we are now ready to look at what seems to be your most fundamental point, your critique of Rationalism as dogmatic, and your alternative of semi-skepticism. Your distinction between impressions and ideas was only a preliminary to this much more fundamental point, and your proof of this fundamental point will need to use your distinction between impressions and ideas. Have I understood your strategy so far?

HUME: You have.

SOCRATES: So here is your main point:

E, II   **Nothing, at first view, may seem more unbounded than the thought of man, which . . . is not even restrained within the limits of nature and reality. To form monsters, and join incongruous shapes and appearances, costs the imagination no more trouble than to conceive the most natural and familiar objects. And while the body is confined to one planet, along which it creeps with pain and difficulty, the thought can in an instant transport us into the most distant regions of the universe, or even beyond the universe. . . . What was never seen, or heard of, may yet be** conceived; nor is any thing beyond the power of thought, except what implies an absolute contradiction.

But though our thought seems to possess this unbounded liberty, we shall find, upon a nearer examination, that it is really confined within very narrow limits, and that all this creative power of the mind amounts to no more than the faculty of compounding, transposing, augmenting, or diminishing the materials afforded us by the senses and experience. When we think of a golden mountain, we only join two consistent ideas; *gold* and *mountain*, with which we were formerly acquainted. A virtuous horse we can conceive; because, from our own feeling, we can conceive virtue, and this we may unite to the figure and shape of a horse, which is an animal familiar to us. In short, all the materials of thinking are derived either from our outward or inward sentiment [sensation, experience]: the mixture and composition of these belongs alone to the mind and will. Or, to express myself in philosophical language, all our ideas or more feeble perceptions are copies of our impressions or more lively ones.

To prove this, the two following arguments will, I hope, be sufficient. First, when we analyze our thoughts or ideas, however compounded or sublime, we always find that they resolve themselves into such simple ideas as were copied from a precedent feeling or

E, II

sentiment [sensation, impression]. Even those
ideas which, at first view, seem the most wide
of this origin, are found, upon a nearer scrutiny, to be derived from it. The idea of God,
as meaning an infinitely intelligent, wise, and
good Being, arises from reflecting on the operations of our own mind and augmenting,
without limit, those qualities of goodness
and wisdom. We may prosecute this enquiry
to what length we please; where we shall always find, that every idea which we examine
is copied from a similar impression. Those
who would assert that this position is not
universally true nor without exception, have
only one, and that an easy method of refuting it; by producing that idea, which, in their
opinion, is not derived from this source. It
will then be incumbent on us, if we would
maintain our doctrine, to produce the impression or lively perception, which corre-
sponds to it.

Secondly. If it happen, from a defect of the
organ, that a man is not susceptible of any
species of sensation, we always find that he
is as little susceptible of the correspondent
ideas. A blind man can form no notion of
colours; a deaf man, of sounds. Restore either of them that sense in which he is deficient; by opening this new inlet for his sensations, you also open an inlet for the ideas;
and he finds no difficulty in conceiving these
objects.

HUME: A long passage to explore, and an important one.

SOCRATES: And so our exploration must also be long, and careful.

HUME: Where do you want to begin?

SOCRATES: With a very general question. The upshot of your whole philosophy is a kind of skepticism, which is a narrowing down of what we know. If you are right, we know far less than we think we do. Is that a fair assessment?

HUME: It is. And you should agree with it, Socrates, for that is the first lesson you always tried to teach to the fools you dialogued with. They always thought they knew, and you always began with Lesson One, that they really knew far less than they thought they did.

SOCRATES: We do seem to be akin there. Whether we really are, is another question—especially since my "Lesson One", as you call it, means that what is real often is very different from what appears to be real.

But here is my very general question: granted that these two things, appearance and reality, differ far more than we usually think they do, as we both agree they do—is that because there is more in appearances than in reality or because there is more in reality than in appearances?

HUME: This is the "Hamlet" question that you raised before, is it not? Whether there are more things in Heaven and earth than are dreamed of in our philosophies, or less? Whether we believe too little or too much?

SOCRATES: Yes. That is the question.

HUME: Perhaps this question can not be meaningfully argued about a priori, before examining each separate instance and example of it.

SOCRATES: Perhaps so. Is this only a "perhaps" to you, or do you claim this is certain?

HUME: It is only a "perhaps".

SOCRATES: Then perhaps it can.

HUME: Perhaps.

SOCRATES: And if it can, then which do you think is more likely? That "there are *more* things in Heaven and earth (that is, in reality) than in your philosophy (that is, in the appearances of reality to your mind)", as Hamlet says, or that there is *less* in reality than in our minds?

HUME: Why do you expect me to render an a priori judgment on this?

SOCRATES: Because I suppose you must say, as a skeptic, that there is less. For that "less" judgment is what I called "the upshot of skepticism", or the anti-Hamlet philosophy?

HUME: Why do you say that this must be "the upshot of skepticism or the anti-Hamlet philosophy"?

SOCRATES: Because your skeptical philosophy narrows reality, at least knowable reality, from what we usually think it is, while Hamlet's philosophy, and

Shakespeare's philosophy, and mine too, expands it. You say that most thoughts are myths to be debunked; but I say that most thoughts are shadows to be followed until we find the realities that cast these shadows. You say that most of what we take for reality are not real things outside the cave of our minds at all, but only shadows on its interior walls. But I say that there is far more "out there" than there is "in here", more in reality than in our cave of appearances.

HUME: I grant you the "upshot". But I deduce this "upshot", my skeptical conclusion, from a long analysis and argumentation. I do not begin with it a priori.

SOCRATES: I realize that.

HUME: Then how do you think we can meaningfully argue about it now a priori, at the beginning? You have some deductive argument up your sleeve, I assume.

SOCRATES: No, I do not. I think we may be able to argue about this by a kind of inductive reasoning instead, by consulting our experience.

HUME: How could you do that?

SOCRATES: By consulting the many instances in our experience of learning something new, or of changing our minds, or of being corrected in our thoughts. If most of these instances seem to fall under one or the other of these two possibilities—if most of them seem to show us that there are fewer things in reality than in our philosophies, then your skeptical conclusion seems probable. But if these experiences usually show us that there are more things in reality than in our philosophies, then your skepticism seems improbable.

HUME: I do not agree with your conclusion that your "expansion" of reality is more likely or probable than my "contraction" of it.

SOCRATES: Why not? What is wrong with my argument for that conclusion?

HUME: You argue from what you call our many instances in experience of finding out that reality is more than we thought. But I deny that these instances are what they seem to be. I say that we are fooled there too, and that when we seemed to have escaped the cave, the narrow scope of our previous thought, we were deluded. Your own philosophy seems a prime example of that delusion to me. I think your "expanded" philosophy is largely fantasy. I further argue that I can *explain* your "expanded" philosophy as fantasy. Your "Platonic Ideas" are a perfect example of it. Because there is a separate *word* for redness, as distinct from red, you and Plato concluded that there is a separate *reality* to redness, as distinct from red things. But not all words refer to realities. So you see, my philosophy explain yours better than yours explains mine.

SOCRATES: If, as you say, ideas are only copies of sense impressions, and sense impressions are only copies of reality, and if copies are always less than their originals, how can any ideas ever even seem to be greater than reality? How can ideas expand to the point of fantasy?

HUME: I clearly explain that in my example of the golden mountain.

SOCRATES: You do. But not many people believe in golden mountains, or even in Platonic Ideas. The example of "Platonic Ideas", by the way, was Plato's idea, not mine. Nor is it an idea of common sense. Common sense does not believe either in "Platonic Ideas" or in your skepticism. It seems to be somewhere between Plato and you. So your examples of golden mountains and Platonic Ideas are not typical. We have not yet talked about the really important things that people typically believe are real and you do not, such as causality, substance, self, free will, life after death, and those kinds of things.

HUME: I am ready to defend my skepticism about each of them in turn.

SOCRATES: But you are ready to defend skepticism in general?

HUME: I am. For I base all my general argument on the same principle as the one on which I base all my particular arguments: the principle that all our ideas are copies of impressions. And copies are less than their originals, not more. Though they may seem to be more, they are not.

SOCRATES: Then we must examine that premise of yours. You say that *all* ideas are copies of impressions?

HUME: Yes indeed. Your Platonic Forms, for instance. Take the Idea of Redness. Redness is only a vague copy of the very vivid red of blood and the vivid red of roses and the vivid red of a cardinal, abstracted from those real instances by the mind, leaving the concrete, vivid reds behind and retaining only a pale, abstract concept of redness. If you do not believe that all ideas are copies of impressions, you must give me an example that contradicts it. Show me an idea that is not copied from an impression.

SOCRATES: What about numbers? Do you believe that numbers are ideas?

HUME: Yes, of course.

SOCRATES: But they are not copies of impressions.

HUME: Yes they are.

SOCRATES: Of what impressions?

HUME: Twoness is copied from what is common to two ducks and two stones and two men, of which we have more vivid impressions.

SOCRATES: And if more vivid, then also more clear?

HUME: Yes.

SOCRATES: But the number two is perfectly clear, more clear than two ducks. Twoness in itself, un-mixed with ducks, is perfectly clear. We can calculate with it. We cannot use ducks instead of numbers to calculate with.

HUME: I suppose I will have to make an exception for mathematical ideas. But not for other ideas, such as the idea of God, and the soul, and the good, and life after death. They are not clear.

SOCRATES: You are skeptical of all such ideas because they are not copied from impressions?

HUME: I am.

SOCRATES: In fact, here is the final skeptical conclusion of the long argument of your book, which begins with this premise that all ideas are copied from impressions. Here is your famous final paragraph:

> **When we run over libraries, persuaded of** E, XII, 3
> **these principles, what havoc must we make?**
> **If we take into our hand any volume; of di-**
> **vinity or school metaphysics, for instance, let**
> **us ask,** *Does it contain any abstract reasoning*
> *concerning quantity or number?* **No.** *Does it*
> *contain any experimental reasoning concerning*
> *matter of fact and existence?* **No. Commit it**
> **then to the flames: for it can contain noth-**
> **ing but sophistry and illusion.**

HUME: You said that paragraph became "famous". I am gratified. *Rightfully* famous, I say.

SOCRATES: "Infamous" would be better.

HUME: Why?

SOCRATES: Because it seems a *reductio ad absurdum* of your premise.

HUME: How?

SOCRATES: You show, with admirably consistent logic, that this conclusion logically follows from your first premise. Now I ask you which is more likely: that the conclusion is false, and therefore the premise also false, or that the premise is true and therefore the conclusion is true?

HUME: That is like asking whether it is more likely that there are more things in Heaven and earth than in our philosophies, or fewer.

SOCRATES: It is. And that is the fundamental difference between you and most others, including myself. You think that religious ideas, such as the idea of God, and metaphysical ideas, such as the idea of being, and substance, and causality, are "sophistry and illusion", are confusions.

HUME: But I explain the confusions clearly and persuasively. I say, for instance, that the idea of God has been formed by augmenting the finite ideas of finite perfections that we find in our experience, and then extending them to infinity, by a kind of extrapolation —rather like a parabola on a graph.

SOCRATES: But clearly this is *not* the origin of the idea of God, if we look at the facts rather than at your theories.

HUME: What facts?

SOCRATES: The minds and lives and writings of religious people, beginning with the most primitive. We always find the idea of God or gods, but we do not find that idea coming from such a sophisticated mental process as you suggest. Instead, we find that the idea comes from what we might call religious experience. These people claim that they have experienced God, or some god, acting, speaking, manifesting Himself to these human minds somehow. In Eastern religions it is usually through mystical experiences. In the Jewish, Christian, and Muslim religions it is through miraculous events and through prophets. In all cases it comes always directly and immediately, never through a process of mental extrapolation, as you say, like a parabola, or any other manipulating of ideas that come from impressions.

HUME: That is how believers describe it, of course. But they are wrong. They are deluded. What is really happening in their minds is what I have described; but their minds are not aware of this process. You might say that their conscious mind is not aware of their unconscious mind. They are deluded.

SOCRATES: About whether God exists?

HUME: About where their idea of God comes from.

SOCRATES: They think it comes from God, or from their meeting God.

HUME: Yes.

SOCRATES: And you say it does not. You say they are deluded.

HUME: Yes.

SOCRATES: Because there is no God? Is that why they are deluded?

HUME: Perhaps. Perhaps they are also deluded about whether God exists. I am not an atheist; I am an agnostic. I do not say I can know that God does not exist. But I say that they cannot know that He does, either.

SOCRATES: But if you explain the origin of the idea of God without any real God, there is no reason for thinking that God is real.

HUME: That is correct. Belief is just that: belief, faith, not reason. But shouldn't we be concentrating on my first principle in epistemology, that all ideas are copies of impressions, rather than concentrating on this one example, the idea of God?

SOCRATES: Indeed we should. Especially since we will come back to the idea of God later, when we explore your rejection of miracles. Let us look then at your two arguments for your first principle of epistemology, that ideas are copies of impressions. Your

E, II   first argument is simply that **"when we analyze our thoughts . . . we always find"** this.

HUME: Yes.

SOCRATES: But that is not an argument at all. It is a summary of the results of an investigation.

HUME: So?

SOCRATES: But you do not supply us with the investigation itself!

HUME: Such an investigation cannot be told in one short paragraph. Only the results of it can be.

SOCRATES: But where is the investigation itself?

HUME: I invite you to make it. And I assure you that this is what you will find.

SOCRATES: "I assure you"—that sounds suspiciously like "bluffing" rather than argument.

HUME: But I give an argument for it. Two of them, in fact. First, if you say that not all ideas are copied from impressions, you must produce an example of such an idea, one not copied from an impression, and if I cannot trace it to an impression, you have refuted me.

SOCRATES: That is indeed an argument. But it is not a good one.

HUME: Why? Because you *can* produce such an example? What is it?

SOCRATES: Perhaps I can, but even if I cannot, this does not seem to me to be a good argument.

HUME: Why not?

SOCRATES: Because it proves nothing. It merely claims that your hypothesis can explain all ideas.

HUME: And if it can, that is quite an accomplishment, is it not?

SOCRATES: I think not.

HUME: Why not?

SOCRATES: Let me try to show you. Suppose I offer another hypothesis to explain all our ideas. Suppose I say that I can trace all your ideas to extraterrestrials, who are hypnotizing you, and suppose I challenge you to refute my hypothesis by producing one idea that cannot be explained by this hypothesis. You will not be able to do it. For whatever idea you produce, I will explain it as part of this hypnosis. No one would say that such an argument proves that all our ideas are in fact produced by extraterrestrial hypnotists. You see, there are always a number of hypotheses that explain the data.

In fact, I could use the very same argument for Rationalism that you use for Empiricism. Both hypotheses explain the data. You trace all ideas to impressions, but I could trace all impressions to ideas. For the very idea of an "impression" is an *idea*. I could reduce trees to the ideas of trees, and red to the idea of red, and pain to the idea of pain, for it is impossible for you to produce anything in your thought that is *not* an idea. For the very act of producing it in thought is the act of making an idea.

You see, it is similar to the argument between the materialist and the spiritualist. The materialist claims that he can explain every supposedly spiritual event in the mind by purely material means. He says that mathematical calculation is only certain electrical impulses in the frontal lobes, and moral ideals are only chemical changes in the medulla oblongata, and so on. But the spiritualist can reply to this "nothing buttery" with his own "nothing buttery". He can say that he can explain every supposed material event by mental and spiritual means. The frontal lobes are only our idea of them, and chemical changes are only our awareness of chemical changes. For the very act of showing you a material thing is a mental act.

HUME: This was Bishop Berkeley's argument. Are you saying that you believe his philosophy that Matter does not exist outside Mind, that all empirical realities are really mental and spiritual?

SOCRATES: Not at all. I am saying that just because one hypothesis can explain all the data, that does not mean it is true. For a different hypothesis can usually be invented that also explains all the data. A hypothesis is not a proof.

HUME: No. But a counterexample to a hypothesis, which the hypothesis cannot explain, is a disproof of the hypothesis.

SOCRATES: That is true.

HUME: And I claim that no one can produce a counterexample to my Empiricist hypothesis. So it cannot be disproved.

SOCRATES: But no one can produce a counterexample to the Rationalist hypothesis either.

HUME: Oh.

SOCRATES: Or to the common-sense hypothesis, halfway between Rationalism and Empiricism, that both sensation and reason, both body and mind, both matter and spirit, are real.

HUME: So we have three equally irrefutable hypotheses. I see why you say I have not resolved the issue with my first argument. But I have a second one.

SOCRATES: Then let me tell you why your second argument also fails to convince me:

If it happen, from a defect of the organ, that a man is not susceptible of any species of sensation, we always find that he is as little susceptible of the correspondent ideas. A blind man can form no notion of colours; a deaf man of sounds. Restore either of them that sense in which he is deficient; by opening this new inlet for his sensations, you also open an inlet for the ideas; and he finds no difficulty in conceiving these objects. E, II

HUME: I think this is an excellent argument against Rationalism. Why does it not seem so to you?

SOCRATES: It does indeed seem to me to be a good argument, because it is an argument from data taken from experience.

HUME: Now you sound like an Empiricist! Well, what do you think is wrong with this argument then? Is it not a valid argument? And does it not refute Rationalism?

SOCRATES: I think the answer to both of those questions is yes. But even if it is a valid argument and refutes Rationalism, it does not prove Empiricism.

HUME: Why not?

SOCRATES: Because at least two hypotheses, not just one, are still left once Rationalism is refuted: your radical Empiricism and common sense moderate Empiricism.

HUME: What do you mean by "moderate Empiricism"?

SOCRATES: I mean the claim that knowledge begins with sensation, as you say, but then rises by abstraction to go beyond it, as you deny. In fact, the argument you give here against Rationalism is almost exactly the same, in words as well as content, as that of St. Thomas Aquinas in the *Summa Theologica*.

HUME: Aquinas and his medieval Scholastic disciples are still much too rationalistic for me. And your Plato even more so.

SOCRATES: He is not *my* Plato. I am here not to defend his philosophy, but to examine yours. And my judgment on yours is that it is more rationalistic than Aquinas or even Plato. In fact, you sound more like Descartes than anyone else.

HUME: What an absurd insult! Where do I say anything that sounds like Descartes, for goodness' sake?

SOCRATES: In the concluding paragraph of your chapter:

> **When we entertain, therefore, any suspicion**   E, II
> **that a philosophical term is employed without any meaning or idea (as is but too frequent), we need but enquire, *from what impression is that supposed idea derived?* And if it be impossible to assign any, this will serve to confirm our suspicion. By bringing ideas into so clear a light, we may reasonably hope to remove all dispute, which may arise, concerning their nature and reality.**

Like Descartes, you claim to remove all disputes by your scientific method. So your goal for philosophy is much higher than mine. Like Descartes, you hope that philosophy, like science, can end all disputes and convince all reasonable minds of its conclusions (though by a very different method than Descartes'). No philosopher ever thought that before Descartes.

So the two of you, the arch-Rationalist and the arch-Empiricist, seem to me really more in agreement, against all previous philosophers, than in disagreement.

HUME: You shock and insult me, Socrates. First you call me a Thomist and then you call me a Cartesian. That is positively inHumean.

SOCRATES: If the label fits, you must wear it.

5

The Division of All Objects of Reason (Things Knowable) into "Relations of Ideas" and "Matters of Fact"

SOCRATES: You call Section IV "Skeptical Doubts concerning the Operations of the Understanding". It seems to me to be the most important section of your book. Do you agree?

HUME: Yes. It makes a difference to everything after it. It is the premise for nearly all my other conclusions.

SOCRATES: How telling it is to hear you use the language of deductive logic, to hear you admit that you argue from "premise" to "conclusions"!

HUME: How else could I argue?

SOCRATES: Inductively, from experience to conclusions. As I remarked before, you seem much more like a Rationalist than an Empiricist.

HUME: Sticks and stones will break my bones, but names will never hurt me.

SOCRATES: But your own words may hurt you. Let's explore some of your words. You seem to make two main points in this section: first, that all objects of human reason are either "relations of ideas" or "matters of fact", and then, second, your critique of the common notion that we can rightly reason by cause and effect.

HUME: Those are indeed my two main points.

SOCRATES: Here is what you say about the first point. (We will save the second for our next conversation.)

E, IV, 1 **All the objects of human reason or enquiry may naturally be divided into two kinds, to wit, *Relations of Ideas* and *Matters of Fact*. Of the first kind are the sciences of Geometry, Algebra, and Arithmetic, and in short, every affirmation which is either intuitively or demonstratively certain. *That the square of the hypothenuse is equal to the square of the two sides*, is a proposition which expresses a relation between these figures. *That three times five is equal to the half of thirty*, expresses a relation between these numbers. Propositions of this kind are discoverable by the mere operation of thought, without dependence on what is anywhere existent in the universe. Though there never were a circle or triangle in nature, the truths demonstrated by Euclid would for ever retain their certainty and evidence.**

Matters of fact, which are the second objects of human reason, are not ascertained

in the same manner; nor is our evidence of their truth, however great, of a like nature with the foregoing. The contrary of every matter of fact is still possible; because it can never imply a contradiction, and is conceived by the mind with the same facility and distinctness, as if ever so conformable to reality. *That the sun will not rise tomorrow* is no less intelligible a proposition, and implies no more contradiction than the affirmation, *that it will rise*. We should in vain, therefore, attempt to demonstrate its falsehood. Were it demonstratively false, it would imply a contradiction, and could never be distinctly conceived by the mind.

You here make three claims, it seems to me. First, that relations of ideas and matters of fact are different, and not overlapping, categories of "things known".

Second, that they are known in totally different ways: that relations of ideas are known by the mind alone, without the senses, while matters of fact are known only by direct sense observation or memory of sense observation.

Third, that there is no third class of "objects of human reason", but that "relations of ideas" and "matters of fact" are the only two kinds.

Is that a fair summary?

HUME: It is indeed.

SOCRATES: Then let us examine these three points one by one. Let us begin with your claim that relations of ideas and matters of fact are exclusive of each other and not overlapping; that no relation of ideas can be a matter of fact and no matter of fact can be a relation of ideas.

HUME: What do you want to know about it?

SOCRATES: I want to know your reason for believing this mutual exclusivity. Is it because our two ways of knowing these two things are totally different and exclusive of each other, matters of fact being known by the senses and relations of ideas being known by the mind?

HUME: That is true, but that is not my reason for believing they are exclusive. For it is logically possible that the things known by the senses could also be known by the mind, and vice versa.

SOCRATES: What is your reason for believing these two to be exclusive, then?

HUME: As I say, **"the contrary of every matter of fact is still possible; because it can never imply a contradiction."** Therefore all matters of fact are uncertain. But "relations of ideas" are certain, because their contrary always implies a contradiction.

SOCRATES: When you say the "contrary" of a proposition, what do you mean?

HUME: The opposite.

SOCRATES: Which proposition would you call the contrary of "all men are mortal"?

HUME: That "not all men are mortal", or "some men are not mortal".

SOCRATES: So what you mean by "contrary" is "contradictory".

HUME: Yes.

SOCRATES: In traditional logic, if we have two universal propositions with the same subject and predicate but one is affirmative and the other is negative, these are called "contraries" rather than "contradictories". For instance, "all men are mortal" and "no men are mortal". But this is not what you mean by "contraries", is it?

HUME: No. I mean contradictories.

SOCRATES: Thank you for that clarification. And what do you mean by "implying a contradiction"?

HUME: There are two ways the contrary—I mean the *contradictory*—of a proposition can logically imply (or, as you would say more properly, logically "entail") a contradiction: immediately or mediately.

By a proposition whose contradiction entails a contradiction *immediately*, and which I call "intuitively certain", I mean a proposition that is self-evident because its contradictory is immediately self-contradictory. Such a proposition is a tautology, like "X is X" or "X is not non-X", or "2 + 2 = 4", or "Whatever has properties x and y, has property y." You know that it is true because its contradictory cannot possibly be true since it is in itself immediately self-contradictory. You need not know anything else to know that X is not non-X, because the contradictory of that proposition, that X *is* non-X, contradicts itself. So "X is not non-X" is "intuitively certain".

By a proposition whose contradiction entails a contradiction *mediately*, I mean a proposition whose contrary (I mean contradictory) implies a contradiction only through the mediation of another proposition, another assumption. The proposition is not immediately self-evident, and its contradiction is not immediately self-contradictory, but the proposition can be proved with the aid of at least one other proposition, simply by the laws of logic, with no reliance on sense experience. For instance "No car of a train can ever be longer, and greater, than the train" can be proved if you add three other propositions: that a car of a train is a part of the train, and that being longer is one way of being greater, and that no part can ever be greater than the whole of which it is a part. These three propositions are also all true by definition, by merely mentally analyzing the meaning of the ideas, and not by learning anything about the real world by sense observation. You don't need to know anything about trains or cars. You could equally well prove that "no gob of a coo can ever be longer than the coo" if you define a gob as part of a coo. You don't need to know what a gob and a coo really are, or even whether they really exist at all.

SOCRATES: I see.

HUME: So "relations of ideas" and "matters of fact" cannot overlap, because either a proposition *can* be proved by the laws of formal logic alone, without knowledge of the real world by sense observation, or it *cannot*.

SOCRATES: And you say that these two kinds of propositions are the only two kinds?

HUME: Yes. That was your third point. You skipped the second one.

SOCRATES: I will come back to it. I want to look at your third point next. Tell me, are the sentences in your book propositions that express something we can know?

HUME: Of course.

SOCRATES: Then they must all be either relations of ideas or matters of fact.

HUME: Yes.

SOCRATES: What about the proposition that all propositions are either relations of ideas or matters of fact? Is that a relation of ideas or a matter of fact?

HUME: That is a relation of ideas. For propositions cannot be seen with the senses.

SOCRATES: I see. And what you call "relations of ideas" can be proved with certainty.

HUME: Yes.

SOCRATES: To everyone's satisfaction. They are like the propositions of geometry rather than like the propositions of ethics or politics or religion.

HUME: Exactly.

SOCRATES: And no one disagrees that $2 + 2 = 4$, or even that $2.22 \times 4.444 = 9.86568$.

HUME: Correct. It just takes a little longer to prove the second than the first.

SOCRATES: And you have discovered this important philosophical principle yourself.

HUME: Yes.

SOCRATES: And you want to teach it to the world.

HUME: Yes.

SOCRATES: Why? Because the world does not yet know it?

HUME: Yes. And because it will dispel much ignorance and confusion.

SOCRATES: But why is there any ignorance and confusion about it, and why does the world not yet know it, and why do other philosophers disagree with it, if as you say it is a relation of ideas and so is self-evident or demonstrable with certainty? Is the world so stupid, are other philosophers so stupid, as not to recognize a certain demonstration when they see one?

HUME: I cannot speak for them, Socrates, but only for myself.

SOCRATES: My question was not really about human minds, about psychology, but about the objects of human minds, about these two kinds of propositions you speak of. Let me be sure I understand what you mean. Let me review your distinction once more, and please correct me if I have misunderstood it in any way. Propositions that you call "relations of ideas" are propositions that can be known to be true just by understanding the meaning of the subject and predicate terms. Is that right?

HUME: Yes.

SOCRATES: So if the predicate is already contained in the subject, or logically implied by the subject, the proposition fits into your class of "relations of ideas".

HUME: Correct.

SOCRATES: That is what Kant will call "analytic propositions".

HUME: Who is Kant?

SOCRATES: A very famous and influential philosopher who will come after you. He was very deeply influenced by you. He will say that you "woke him from his dogmatic slumber". And your second kind of proposition, which you call a "matter of fact", is what Kant will call a "synthetic proposition". The predicate of a synthetic proposition is *not* already contained in its subject.

HUME: And that is why there can be only two kinds of propositions: because there are only two possibilities: either the predicate is or is not already contained in the meaning of the subject.

SOCRATES: But Kant will say there are *four* kinds of propositions, not just two, because there are two *standards* by which we can classify propositions: one is the relation between the meaning of the predicate and the meaning of the subject, as we have seen, and the other is how we come to know the proposition. Propositions we know to be true only after sense experience he will call "a posteriori" propositions because they are known to be true only posterior to experience. Propositions that we know to be true before sense experience he will call "a priori" propositions because they can be known to be true prior to sense experience.

HUME: But this standard of classifying propositions still gives us only two kinds of propositions, Socrates. For all analytic propositions are a priori and all synthetic propositions are a posteriori. I have included both standards of classification in my division, for I say that "relations of ideas" are known prior to sensation and that "matters of fact" are known only posterior to sensation. Why did Kant use two standards? The two result in the same identical classification.

SOCRATES: Because he thought they did not, and that a third kind of proposition was possible, namely synthetic a priori propositions, propositions that were not analytic, not just tautologies, not just relations of ideas, and yet could be known prior to experience.

HUME: There are no such propositions. That is why I was a skeptic of all metaphysics and theology and much of traditional philosophy, even ethics: I insisted that these pseudo-sciences could have no real meaning, no cognitive content, because they contained this third kind of proposition, and this kind of proposition is a simple confusion. How could there be synthetic a priori propositions? How could any matters of fact be known prior to our experience of the facts that they state? How could we know a priori that the sky is blue or that the sun will rise tomorrow, prior to experiencing it? How could we know it rather than just opine it, or believe it? How could we know it with certainty rather than mere probability? Clearly, we cannot.

SOCRATES: And your reason for believing that we cannot is . . . ?

HUME: As I said, "because the contrary of a matter of fact can never imply a contradiction." It is not self-contradictory to deny that the sky is blue, as it is contradictory to deny that blue is blue or that the sky is sky. It is false, but it is not self-contradictory, and therefore we can know it only by observing the sky, not merely by examining the ideas of "sky" and "blue". I do not see how Kant or anyone else could think that there could possibly be a third kind of proposition. Give me an example of such a proposition. Would it be an example from the old superstition of metaphysics? I do not see how you can say that this fellow Kant was influenced by me, or that I awoke him from his dogmatic slumber, if he simply reverted back to the old metaphysics.

SOCRATES: No, Kant also denied that the old metaphysics was possible. But he thought he found a new kind of metaphysics. But I will not give you an example from Kant, for we are not discussing his philosophy here today. Instead, I will give you an example from common sense. Let us take the proposition "all men are mortal." How would you classify that?—as a "relation of ideas" or as a "matter of fact"?

HUME: As a matter of fact. For it can be denied without self-contradiction. We can conceive of a man who is not mortal, though in fact there is no such man. To show that we can conceive of this, all we have to do is to read the story in the Bible, the story of Adam, the first man, who according to the story was created immortal, but who contracted the disease of death after he ate the forbidden fruit. Now mind you, I do not say that this story is true, that it really happened; but it is meaningful, it can be believed, and many people do believe it. So it is not *self-contradictory*. For self-contradictions are meaningless, and what is meaningless simply cannot be believed by anyone, no matter how credulous or foolish they may be. One simply cannot tell a story, or believe a story, about a man who was simultaneously mortal and immortal, any more than one can tell or believe a story about a sun that simultaneously did and did not rise. But one can tell a story about a man who was once immortal and then became mortal, just as one can tell a story about a sun that for a long time did not rise and then did rise.

SOCRATES: I see. You make that very clear. So you say that "all men are mortal" can be known to be true only after experience.

HUME: Of course.

SOCRATES: What experience?

HUME: The experience of seeing other men die, of course.

SOCRATES: And how many men have you seen die?

HUME: With my own eyes? A few dozen.

SOCRATES: You have not seen *all* men.

HUME: Of course not. Most of them died before I was born or were born after I died.

SOCRATES: So there is no way for you to know that *all* men are mortal.

HUME: Exactly.

SOCRATES: Then how do you know that you will die, if you have not yet experienced your own death? Surely you don't believe that you can deduce it from the general principle that "all men are mortal", since you say you can know that general principle only by experience, since that general principle is not a "relation of ideas" but a "matter of fact".

HUME: Quite so. I don't claim to know that I will die! I believe it, but I do not know it. It is probable, but not certain. "All men are mortal" is not knowable as a certainty because all men are not experienceable by any one man. And it is not a relation of ideas because there is no contradiction in denying it. So I do *not* know with certainty that all men are mortal.

SOCRATES: Nor that you are mortal?

HUME: No.

SOCRATES: And yet you make funeral preparations, and you write your will. You count on dying.

HUME: I do not count on it; I bet on it. It is extremely probable.

SOCRATES: But not certain.

HUME: Right.

SOCRATES: So you risk being wrong.

HUME: Right.

SOCRATES: You risk the remote possibility that you will never die.

HUME: Right.

SOCRATES: You do not risk a self-contradiction.

HUME: No.

SOCRATES: But you do risk a miracle.

HUME: I do not believe in miracles either.

SOCRATES: But they are *possible*, for they do not involve a self-contradiction.

HUME: No, I believe they are not possible. As I show later in my book.

SOCRATES: Then you contradict yourself in this one instance of miracles.

HUME: How?

SOCRATES: You say you have no knowledge of any universal truths beyond your experience, such as that all men are mortal, and yet you say that you do have knowledge of this one universal truth beyond your experience, namely, that in all the history of the world, in all the ages before your life and all the ages after your life, and in all the nations and peoples of this large world, that there never has been and never will be a miracle.

HUME: No, I do not say that it is certain that there are no miracles. It is still only an argument from experience, though the experience is the experience of the uniformity of nature, which is an an experience that all men have at all times. So the conclusion is extremely probable, but only probable, not certain.

SOCRATES: Ah, so you are not *certain* that there are no miracles.

HUME: Not quite. But it is as close to certainty as any argument from experience can ever get.

SOCRATES: We must postpone investigating your argument against miracles now, for we have not yet understood your basic premises, especially your claim that all that we can know fits into these two classes, "relations of ideas" and "matters of fact". To return to our example of "all men are mortal", then: Do you say that we cannot know this with certainty?

HUME: That is what I say.

SOCRATES: Because it is not a "relation of ideas".

HUME: Yes.

SOCRATES: But most people would say that it *is* both a "relation of ideas" *and* a "matter of fact", and that we can know it with certainty.

HUME: But how? I challenge them to answer that question.

SOCRATES: Let me take up their position, then, so that you can spar with another mind that is present, not just with an idea that is absent. I think they would answer your question this way: they would say that they could know that all men are mortal neither by the law of noncontradiction alone, which a computer can also do, nor by sense observation, which a camera can also do, but by *understanding*, which only a human being can do. They would say that your division of all knowledge into relations of ideas and matters of fact implicitly reduces man to a computer plus a camera.

HUME: But how do they know that all men are mortal?

SOCRATES: By understanding the meaning of the terms "man" and "mortal". And this is how they would call it a "relation of ideas", I think. They would say that "man" necessarily means "rational animal", and that "animal" necessarily means "organic body", and that "organic body" necessarily means "living only by the operation and cooperation of the material organs", and that these organs could fail to operate or cooperate, and that this is what death means; and therefore that if we understand the meaning of "man" we can understand that all men are mortal not by accident but by essence, and necessarily, and therefore certainly.

HUME: So they would say that "all men are mortal" is a "relation of ideas".

SOCRATES: Not in the sense that you mean it: they would agree with you that it is not self-contradictory to deny it. Thus the story in the Bible of Adam and Eve in the state of immortality, whether true or false, is not self-contradictory.

HUME: Then how do they claim to *know* that all men are mortal?

SOCRATES: By *understanding* the ideas of "men" and "mortal", or rather by understanding the realities designated by the ideas, the reality of human nature and the reality of mortality.

HUME: And I deny that those are realities at all!

SOCRATES: Why do you deny that?

HUME: Because "man" and "mortal" are universals, not particulars.

SOCRATES: I see. Your Nominalism is really at the root of your whole philosophy.

HUME: And will you now insist on a metaphysical discussion of the old issue of universals?

SOCRATES: No, my task is confined to exploring your book. But in doing so I find it useful to smoke out your hidden premises, one of which is Nominalism. And it is also useful to smoke out your hidden *consequences*, especially the consequences of this key point of yours, the reduction of all objects of human reason to "relations of ideas" and "matters of fact".

HUME: You mean the *logical* consequences.

SOCRATES: Yes, but also the *historical* consequences. For a philosophy will arise almost two centuries after yours that will powerfully influence and even dominate the vast majority of all English-speaking philosophers throughout most of the twentieth century, and the central contention of this philosophy will be almost exactly your point here about there being only two objects of human reason. The philosophy will be called Logical Positivism, in its earlier and simpler form. A man named A. J. Ayer will write a book called *Language, Truth and Logic*, which will be the Bible of the movement. Later versions of this philosophy will modify and soften its simple claims, and the name will change to something more generic— "analytic philosophy"—but the basic thrust of the philosophy will remain Humean. Instead of speaking about "objects of human reason", this philosophy will speak of the "meaning of propositions". And it will contend that the meaning of a proposition is its mode of verification.

HUME: What, exactly, do they mean by "verification"? Proof?

SOCRATES: Yes, if "proof" is extended to mean not only "proof of certainty" but also "proof of probability". And if it is extended to mean "falsification" or "disproof" as well as proof.

HUME: But is this not a confusion between what a proposition *means* and how we know it is *true*?

SOCRATES: Perhaps. But its point is that if we do not even know how it would be possible ever, in principle, to verify or falsify a certain proposition, then that proposition does not have any intelligible meaning. It is meaningless.

HUME: That seems correct. If you claim, for instance, that there is an invisible entity in this room that cannot ever be seen or heard, under any conditions, then it makes no difference whether I agree or disagree with your claim, for it is unverifiable.

SOCRATES: That is what their "verification principle" says. And they then go on to say, as you do, that there are only two kinds of meaningful propositions (which correspond to your two kinds of objects of reason): empirically verifiable propositions and tautologies. Empirically verifiable propositions are what you call "matters of fact" and tautologies are what you call "relations of ideas".

HUME: This philosophy still sounds right so far.

SOCRATES: Empirically verifiable (or falsifiable) propositions are—well, empirically verifiable (or falsifiable). They took "empirical" in a rather broad sense, as you did, so that it could include our awareness of our own inner states of mind, such as feelings and desires. It is meaningful to say I feel depressed now, even though my five external senses do not perceive it.

HUME: Go on. I see nothing wrong so far. What about the other kind of meaningful proposition?

SOCRATES: Tautologies are verifiable by the law of noncontradiction alone, for the contradictory of such a proposition always implies a contradiction. All the propositions of mathematics are tautologies or reducible to tautologies.

HUME: What about the propositions of the physical sciences?

SOCRATES: The propositions of the physical sciences are combinations of the empirical and the mathematical. So they are meaningful.

HUME: This sounds exactly like what I say.

SOCRATES: But nearly all philosophers came to see that this philosophy was itself self-contradictory.

HUME: How?

SOCRATES: By a very simple argument. And this simple argument seems to refute both their "verification principle" and your earlier version of it, on which theirs was based.

HUME: What is this "simple argument"?

SOCRATES: That by its own criterion, the "verification principle" is meaningless. For it claims that all propositions that are not empirically verifiable or tautological are meaningless. But the "verification principle" itself is neither empirically verifiable nor tautological. Therefore it must be meaningless—as meaningless as the propositions of metaphysics, theology, ethics, and aesthetics that it excludes because they are not empirically verifiable or tautological.

HUME: Why isn't the "verification principle" empirically verifiable?

SOCRATES: Because we neither sense nor feel propositions. We do not experience propositions. Propositions are not matters of fact, like turtles, or storms.

HUME: Of course not.

SOCRATES: But the principle is not tautological either. It is not possible to think or believe the contradictory of a tautology. But it is possible to think and to believe the contradictory of the "verification principle". In fact, most philosophers have thought and believed exactly that. Not you, perhaps, but all or nearly all philosophers before you.

HUME: That is why I consign their books to the flames!

SOCRATES: Exactly as the Logical Positivists did. But they would have to consign their own books to the flames then, for their basic principle is meaningless by its own standards. You cannot see or feel any propositions, and therefore you cannot see or feel that proposition that they called the "verification principle". But you cannot prove it by the law of noncontradiction either. It is not a tautology, like $2 + 2 = 4$ or $x = x$.

HUME: This "simple argument" sounds like the argument against simple skepticism: it is self-contradictory to say that I know that I know nothing.

SOCRATES: Yes. And it seems that all softened or sophisticated forms of skepticism are similarly vulnerable to self-contradiction, such as "I am certain that no knowledge is certain, only probable", or "I know as an objective matter of fact that no one can know any objective matter of fact", or "It is absolutely true that there are no absolute truths", or "It is a universal truth that no truths are universal", or "It is a necessary and unchangeable truth that truth is not necessary and unchangeable."

HUME: But I am not that kind of a skeptic, a simple, absolute, or Phyrrhonian skeptic. I am an academic skeptic, a scientific skeptic, a suspender of judgment.

SOCRATES: And just as you softened skepticism, later analytic philosophers similarly softened the verification principle. But they did not add a third kind of meaningful proposition. They did not explain how to bring back the old metaphysics, the old wisdom. And neither did you. But we will explore your "softened" skepticism later, when we come to it in your book.

6

The Critique of Causality

SOCRATES: The next point we should investigate is probably your most famous point of all.

HUME: My critique of causality?

SOCRATES: Yes. It comes in Section IV, the section you call "Skeptical Doubts concerning the Operations of the Understanding". It is probably your most powerful argument for your most fundamental skeptical conclusion, for it has probably caused more readers to become skeptics than anything else you ever wrote.

HUME: If skepticism logically follows from my premises, then so be it.

SOCRATES: Well, let us see whether it does or whether it doesn't. That is indeed your claim. In fact, the single most important word in this section, I think, is the word "therefore", which connects your critique of causality, as your conclusion, with your previous point about the classifying of all things knowable into "relations of ideas" and "matters of fact", as your premise, when you write:

It may, therefore, be a subject worthy of cu- E, IV, 1
riosity, to enquire what is the nature of that

**evidence which assures us of any real exis-
tence of matter of fact, beyond the present
testimony of our senses, of the records of our
memory.**

Do I interpret you correctly if I say that here you
ask the following question: If you are right in saying
that all we can know is "relations of ideas" and "matters of fact", and if the only way to know "matters
of fact" is by sense observation, since the opposite of
a "matter of fact" can never imply a contradiction,
then why do most people *believe* that they can have
certain knowledge of matters of fact that are not simply present or past sense observation?

HUME: That is precisely my question.

SOCRATES: And here is precisely your answer. In one
word, it is "causality".

E, IV, 1   **All reasonings concerning matter of fact seem
to be founded on the relation of *Cause and
Effect*. By means of that relation alone we can
go beyond the evidence of our memory and
senses. If you were to ask a man, why he believes any matter of fact, which is absent, for
instance, that his friend is in the country, or
in France, he would give you a reason; and
this reason would be some other fact, as a
letter received from him, or the knowledge
of his former resolutions and promises. A
man finding a watch or any other machine in
a desert island would conclude that there had
once been men in that island. All our reasonings concerning fact are of the same nature.**

And here it is constantly supposed that there is a connexion between the present fact and that which is inferred from it. Were there nothing to bind them together, the inference would be entirely precarious. The hearing of an articulate voice and rational discourse in the dark assures us of the presence of a person: Why? because these are the *effects* of the human . . .

If we would satisfy ourselves, therefore, concerning the nature of that evidence, which assures us of matters of fact, we must enquire how we arrive at the knowledge of cause and effect.

HUME: You said, quite rightly, that "therefore" was the most important word in my argument. Are you going to disagree with it now? Do you think my conclusion does not follow, that the connection is not as logically tight as I say it is?

SOCRATES: No, your connection seems perfectly clear and correct here.

HUME: So what is left to investigate?

SOCRATES: Your answer to your question, of course. As you say, "we must enquire how we arrive at the knowledge of cause and effect." That "enquiry" is the heart of your *Enquiry*.

And here it is, perhaps the most crucial passage in your whole book:

I shall venture to affirm, as a general proposition, which admits of no exception, that the

knowledge of this relation is not, in any instance, attained by reasonings *a priori*; but
arises entirely from experience, when we find
that any particular objects are constantly conjoined with each other. Let an object be presented to a man of ever so strong natural reason and abilities; if that object be entirely
new to him, he will not be able, by the most
accurate examination of its sensible qualities,
to discover any of its causes or effects. Adam,
though his rational faculties be supposed, at
the very first, entirely perfect, could not have
inferred from the fluidity and transparency
of water that it would suffocate him, or from
the light and warmth of fire that it would
consume him. No object ever discovers, by
the qualities which appear to the senses, either the causes which produced it, or the effects which will arise from it; nor can our
reason, unassisted by experience, ever draw
any inference concerning real existence and
matter of fact.

E, IV   . . . *Causes and effects are discoverable not by
reason but by experience.* . . .

We fancy that were we brought on a sudden into this world, we could at first have inferred that one billiard-ball would commu-
nicate motion to another upon impulse; and
that we needed not to have waited for the
event, in order to pronounce with certainty
concerning it. Such is the influence of custom, that, where it is the strongest, it not

only covers our natural ignorance but even conceals itself. . . .

The mind can never possibly find the effect in the supposed cause, by the most accurate scrutiny and examination. For the effect is totally different from the cause, and consequently can never be discovered in it. Motion in the second billiard-ball is a quite distinct event from motion in the first, nor is there anything in the one to suggest the smallest hint of the other. . . .

And as the first imagination or invention of a particular effect, in all natural operations, is arbitrary, where we consult not experience; so must we also esteem the supposed tie or connexion between the cause and effect, which binds them together, and renders it impossible that any other effect could result from the operation of that cause. When I see, for instance, a billiard-ball moving in a straight line towards another, even suppose motion in the second ball should by accident be suggested to me, as the result of their contact or impulse; may I not conceive, that a hundred different events might as well follow from that cause? May not both these balls remain at absolute rest? May not the first ball return in a straight line, or leap off from the second in any line or direction? All these suppositions are consistent and conceivable. Why then should we give the preference to one, which is no more consistent or conceivable than the rest? All our reasonings *a priori* will never be able to show us any foundation for this preference.

In a word, then, every effect is a distinct event from its cause. It could not, therefore, be discovered in the cause, and the first invention or conception of it, *a priori*, must be entirely arbitrary. And even after it is suggested, the conjunction of it with the cause must appear equally arbitrary; since there are always many other effects, which, to reason, must seem fully as consistent and natural. In vain, therefore, should we pretend to determine any single event, or infer any cause or effect, without the assistance of observation and experience.

E, IV, I   Hence we may discover the reason why no philosopher, who is rational and modest has ever pretended to assign the ultimate cause of any natural operation, or to show distinctly the action of that power, which produces any single effect in the universe. It is confessed, that the utmost effort of human reason is to reduce the principles, productive of natural phenomena, to a greater simplicity, and to resolve the many particular effects into a few general causes, by means of reasonings from analogy, experience, and observation. But as to the causes of these general causes, we should in vain attempt their discovery; nor shall we ever be able to satisfy ourselves, by any particular explication of them. These ultimate springs and princi-

**ples are totally shut up from human curios-
ity and enquiry.**

HUME: That is a very long and copious passage you
have quoted, Socrates. I wonder whether we will have
the time to examine it adequately.

SOCRATES: Oh, I think you need not fret about *that*,
David. In this place, time is generated by need rather
than need constricted by time. If we want the time,
we have it.

HUME: Was the great Newton wrong then about time
being an absolute?

SOCRATES: He was wrong even in the physical order.

HUME: Can you explain this to me? As a scientist, I
am very curious.

SOCRATES: I will try to satisfy your curiosity just a
little, as a bit of mental refreshment, rather like taking a breath of air before we plunge into the waters
of our analysis of this long and difficult passage about
causality.

An even greater scientific mind than Newton, a
man named Albert Einstein, will prove more than a
century later that time is relative to matter in motion; that time is rather like the scent thrown off by
an animal as it runs: the larger the animal and the
faster it runs, the more scent there is.

But even before Einstein, and even before Newton, men knew that there were two kinds of time, not
just one; that physical time, whether it was absolute,
as Newton thought, or relative, as Einstein proved,
was not the most primordial kind of time. For unless

we first *experienced* time in our lives—those lives that are neither purely physical nor purely mental—we could never have formed the purely mental abstract *concept* of merely physical time to measure the merely motion of merely physical bodies. And in the world we all lived in as children, before we ever learned any physical science or even learned how to tell time by chronometers and clocks, we experienced a more primordial kind of time, a kind of time that was more subjective and qualitative rather than objective and quantitative time; our *kairos*, as we Greeks used to say, was constricted and constrained by *kronos*, or clock time, the time we invented in our minds to measure the purely physical world. Then, when we became adults, we succumbed to the rule of *kronos*. We let ourselves be enslaved by our own invention. We kept saying "there is not enough time", when we ourselves had invented it.

But that was then and this is now. In this world, after death, we are no longer that foolish. Here, there are no clocks but inner clocks. Here, time is measured by need.

HUME: I would dearly love to investigate the relation between these two kinds of time further, if there is enough time now.

SOCRATES: There is, but not now.

HUME: I thought you said there was always plenty of time here.

SOCRATES: There is. But only for what is needed. Here, it is our real human need that causes physical time to expand or contract. And what we need to do now is to examine your argument about causality.

HUME: You speak of a causality that is not between two physical events, but between time itself and human need: a causality between two kinds of causality! I would dearly desire to investigate *that* concept too. . . .

SOCRATES: All in good time, David. But since time is determined by need here, and since our need now is to explore your book's discussion about physical causality first, and not to generate a new discussion, and perhaps a new book, about the relation between the two kinds of time, or about the two kinds of causality, it follows that we must finish your book first. For though the laws of time are changed here, the laws of logic are not.

HUME: I must accept your authority here, Socrates.

SOCRATES: It is a higher authority that you must accept, David, of which I am only the instrument, in this world just as I was in the older one.

HUME: Do you mean . . . ?

SOCRATES: There will be plenty of time for those higher and deeper questions in good time, David. For now, we need to unravel your famous critique of causality, for you have entangled many philosophers in its skeptical fetters, we need to see whether we can release them.

Let us begin by distinguishing the different claims you make.

First, you say that the only way we can know any matter of fact that we do not directly perceive with our senses is by causality, by causal connection, by reasoning from cause to effect or effect to cause.

Second, you say that the connection between the premise and the conclusion in such reasoning depends on the connection between cause and effect in fact.

Third, you say that the only justification for causal reasoning is custom or habit; that we observe a "constant conjunction" of two events, and we assume that they are causally related.

So it is only sense experience plus custom that justifies causal reasoning. Here is where you give your famous billiard balls as an illustration.

Fourth, you say that every effect is a distinct event from its cause, and that is why reason can never discover an effect just by knowing its cause. Only sense experience can discover this.

Fifth, you say that for this reason, natural science never has discovered and never will discover unobservable ultimate causes, or first causes.

Is that a fair summary?

HUME: It is.

SOCRATES: Which of these five claims do you think most philosophers, and for that matter most non-philosophers too, will find radical and controversial, and which do you think they will find acceptable and commonsensical?

HUME: I think they will find all of them radical if they think carefully, for they are all bound up with each other. They are a "package deal".

SOCRATES: But don't you think most people would agree with your first two principles, that it is only by causal reasoning that we can know matters of fact that we do not sense, and that the justification for the logical connection between premise and conclusion in causal reasoning is the real, physical connection between cause and effect in the real world?

HUME: Well, perhaps so. But those are just my preliminary points. The bite of my critique is in the other three points.

SOCRATES: But your fifth and last principle—that science cannot discover first causes—don't you think most people would agree with that too?

HUME: Indeed not. For they have a religious stake in this idea: that there is an ultimate cause, a God, and they believe that God is a "matter of fact" even though He can never be observed with the senses; and therefore they very much want to believe that science gives us reasons for believing in God.

SOCRATES: But surely this reasoning is a philosophical argument rather than a scientific one. Surely you do not think that most people think that *science* rather than philosophy is going to prove the existence of God.

HUME: Oh, but I think many people *do* believe that.

SOCRATES: Then I think you are tilting at windmills, or straw men, if *that* idea is your opponent. For that idea seems not only false but silly. Do you really think most people expect God to show up in a test tube some day?

HUME: No, but most people expect that what does show up in test tubes will prove God.

SOCRATES: How?

HUME: By causal reasoning.

SOCRATES: But why would anyone need test tubes, or science, for that? How could science do anything more than tell us more about the material world that furnishes all its data? Whether we simply see the planets move across the sky or whether we understand the true astronomical causes of their motion, in either case the philosophical argument for the existence of God as an Unmoved Mover from the premise of the existence of moved movers is in exactly the same state. The validity of the argument does not depend on the complexity of its premise.

HUME: You and I understand that, Socrates, but I doubt that most people do.

SOCRATES: I think you underestimate the common rational sense of most people. But that is not what we are investigating—the reason of "most people" —but only the reason of David Hume. So I think we should turn from principles One and Two and Five to the other two, which will prove much more controversial.

HUME: Fine. Let us move to my billiard table, then.

SOCRATES: Ah, but perhaps it is that move that is the questionable step. I mean the assumption that all causal relations are like the relations between two events on the billiard table. Do you think your critique would stand up just as well if you used a different example of causality? For instance, the causal relation between a mother and her baby? Or between the teaching of a teacher and the learning of his student? Or between happiness and a smile? Or between a mind understanding one idea and that mind understanding another idea that is implied in the first one? For we use the word "cause" to explain all four relationships. We say the baby was born *because* of the mother, and we say the student learned *because* of the teacher, and we say that someone is smiling *because* he is happy, and we say that we understand that we must be mortal *because* we understand what physical organic bodies are. All four of these examples seem to be examples of causal reasoning, yet they seem quite different from your example of one billiard ball hitting another. So I wonder whether your choice of an example is representative enough, typical enough, and whether what you say would follow if you used these other examples instead.

HUME: If those are examples of causality, then they must exemplify the same general principles about causality that I used my billiard balls to explain.

SOCRATES: Well, then, let us see whether or not they do. Suppose we substituted "mother" and "baby", or "teaching" and "learning", or "happiness" and "smile", or "understanding bodies" and "understanding mortality" for your "motion in the first billiard ball" and "motion in the second". Would what you say still make sense? Let us take your fourth point first: Are these two things totally distinct events, as you say cause and effect always are?

HUME: In one sense they are not. Once the baby is born, the mother is continually and always the mother of the baby, and the child is the child of the mother. The cause and effect here operate simultaneously, like an iron ball making a round depression in the pillow it rests on. And that is also true for happiness causing a smile: we are not first happy and then we smile, but we smile as long as we are happy. But the motions of the two billiard balls are not simultaneous but separated in time. I know of that distinction: Aristotle distinguished those two kinds of causality, and Thomas Aquinas argued that God's causal relation to the world was of the second kind rather than the first: that He constantly held up the world, as a table holds up a book, rather than creating it and then falling asleep, as the deists say He did. I do not involve myself in such theological disputes. But I think my principles work just as well for the simultaneous kind of causality as for the billiard-ball type. For if you had never *seen* babies come from mothers, or eggs come from birds, you would not be able to predict then. The sense experience of the cause and of the effect are quite different. You do not see the baby in the mother (unless you peer into her womb) or the egg in the bird, so if you had never seen it happen before, you would never be able to predict these two births. You predict them on the basis of experiencing a constant conjunction of these two distinct things, not on the basis of a priori reasoning.

SOCRATES: I think I see your point. It is the point made by a later philosopher, G. K. Chesterton, who agreed with this principle but not with the skeptical conclusions you drew from it. Let me quote him, from the chapter in *Orthodoxy*[1] called "The Ethics of Elfland", and see whether you are saying what he is saying: "My first and last philosophy . . . are the things called fairy tales. They seem to me to be the entirely reasonable things. . . ."

HUME: That does not sound like a very promising beginning.

SOCRATES: Be patient and listen, and I think you will hear an eloquent echo of your own insight.

> It might be stated this way. There are certain   O, IV
> sequences or developments (cases of one thing
> following another), which are, in the true sense
> of the word, reasonable. They are, in the true
> sense of the word, necessary. Such are math-
> ematical and merely logical sequences. We in
> fairyland (who are the most reasonable of all
> creatures) admit that reason and that necessity.
> For instance, if the Ugly Sisters are older than
> Cinderella, it is (in an iron and awful sense) *nec-
> essary* that Cinderella is younger than the Ugly
> Sisters.

HUME: That is what I call a "relation of ideas".

SOCRATES: Yes. Now see how he contrasts what "matters of fact".

> But as I put my head over the hedge of the   O, IV
> elves and began to take notice of the natural

---

[1] Gilbert Keith Chesterton, *Orthodoxy*, © 1908 John Lane Com-
pany, London (Reprinted in 1995 by Ignatius Press, San Francisco).
Quotations from *Orthodoxy* are indicated as O in the sidenotes.

world, I observed an extraordinary thing. I observed that learned men in spectacles were talk-
ing of the actual things that happened—dawn
and death and so on—as if *they* were rational
and inevitable. They talked as if the fact that
trees bear fruit were just as *necessary* as the fact
that two and one trees make three. But it is
not. There is an enormous difference by the test
of fairyland, which is the test of the imagination. You cannot *imagine* two and one not making three. But you can easily imagine trees not
growing fruit; you can imagine them growing
golden candlesticks or tigers hanging on by the
tail. . . . We have always in our fairy tales kept
this sharp distinction between the science of
mental relations, in which there really are laws,
and the science of physical facts, in which there
are no laws, but only weird repetitions. We believe in bodily miracles, but not in mental im-
possibilities. . . .

[W]e cannot say why an egg can turn into a
chicken any more than we can say why a bear
could turn into a fairy prince. As *ideas*, the egg
and the chicken are further off [from] each other
than the bear and the prince; for no egg in itself suggests a chicken, whereas some princes do
suggest bears. . . . When we are asked why eggs
turn to birds or fruits fall in autumn, we must answer exactly as the fairy godmother would answer if Cinderella asked her why mice turned
to horses or her clothes fell from her at twelve
o'clock. We must answer that it is *magic*. It is

not a "law," for we do not understand its general formula. It is not a necessity, for though we can count on it happening practically, we have no right to say that it must always happen. . . . We do not count on it; we bet on it. We risk the remote possibility of a miracle. . . .

I deny altogether that this is fantastic or even mystical. . . . It is the only way I can express in words my clear and definite perception that one thing is quite distinct from another; that there is no logical connection between flying and laying eggs. It is the man who talks about a "law" that he has never seen who is the mystic. . . . He is a sentimentalist in this essential sense, that he is soaked and swept away by mere associations. He has so often seen birds fly and lay eggs that he feels as if there must be some dreamy, tender connection between the two ideas, whereas there is none.

HUME: That is precisely my point, put with much more rhetorical skill than I could put it.

SOCRATES: And I think most people would agree with it—

HUME: Oh. I thought you were going to contest it.

SOCRATES: —but not with the skeptical conclusions that you draw from it.

HUME: Well, that is because they are not as logical as I am.

SOCRATES: Perhaps. But perhaps your examples are still skewered. Surely the relation between two events that are not purely physical, like teaching and learning, or understanding one idea and understanding another, are related in a different way than billiard balls.

HUME: I do not see why that must be so at all.

SOCRATES: Because when one billiard ball hits another, its impetus, or kinetic energy, ceases when it hits the second, and then, instantly, the second ball *gains* kinetic energy. There seems to be a quantitative transfer of physical energy, which we can calculate mathematically. If the first ball is big enough, or moves fast enough, it can move the second one ten feet, but if not, not. The effect can gain only as much as the cause loses.

HUME: I do not accept your analysis of causality even among billiard balls. I am skeptical of all mysterious and invisible forces like "energy", and I maintain that this notion of some mysterious transfer of energy between moving bodies is wholly unverifiable, common as it is even among physical scientists.

SOCRATES: Well, if it is unverifiable, how is it so perfectly measurable? But let that point go: I am not investigating the idea that there exists an invisible energy now, or that it is transferred from one body to another.

HUME: What point are you investigating?

SOCRATES: Whether the causal relationship, whatever it is, is the same when it occurs between billiard balls and when it occurs between minds. I think it is not. For in the case of causality between minds, the case of teaching and learning, the teacher does not lose any wisdom or knowledge when he shares it with his student, as the first billiard ball loses energy, or momentum, when it hits the second.

HUME: Oh. That is obviously true. And how do you explain that?

SOCRATES: I explain it very simply. Clearly, physical powers are very different than spiritual powers. For physical goods are competitive and diminish when shared, but spiritual goods not only do not diminish when shared but actually multiply. The more money or food or space I give you, the less I have left for myself. But the more I teach you or love you, the more I teach and love myself. Sharing truth or love —which is a kind of nonphysical causality—does not diminish the truth or love in the sharer. The effect does not drain the cause. Nor can it be measured quantitatively or predicted accurately, as it can with the billiard balls, so that is a second difference. If you admit these differences, I wonder how you account for them.

HUME: I do not speak of mysterious, invisible spiritual forces.

SOCRATES: I know. That is precisely your problem.

HUME: No, it is part of my solution.

SOCRATES: But it simply ignores, instead of explaining, these two "matters of fact" that actually exist, and that register on our experience—on everyone's experience. Your metaphysics prohibits you from giving an explanation of them. You are a materialist, and you simply cannot explain immaterial things like wisdom or love. So you ignore or deny them. You are a reductionist. First, you reduce all experience to sense experience, and, second, you reduce all reason to scientific, calculating, mathematical reason.

HUME: But that is exactly the scientific method.

SOCRATES: Yes, it is. But is the scientific method a *fact*?

HUME: What do you mean?

SOCRATES: Is it something like a tree, that registers on the senses?

HUME: No, it is the way of explaining anything that registers on the senses.

SOCRATES: And does it occur in nature, like a rainstorm?

HUME: Of course not.

SOCRATES: Where does it come from?

HUME: The human mind, of course.

SOCRATES: Yes. We made it up. It is an artificial thing.

HUME: So what?

SOCRATES: Well, we may not know how nature or God made up trees, because we are not nature and we are not God. But since we made up this method, we should know how we did it.

HUME: Of course we do. I still don't see your point.

SOCRATES: Just follow me one more step, please, if you will. Here is how we made up this wonderful artifice that we call the scientific method. We wanted to explain and control nature, so we invented a means to that end.

HUME: True.

SOCRATES: And here is how we invented it. It was produced by abstraction.

HUME: Abstraction? Why do you call it an abstraction?

SOCRATES: Because any abstraction abstracts a part from a whole. Is that not what we mean by abstraction, a "taking-away", or *ab-straho*?

HUME: Yes, that is the literal meaning of the word. I still don't see what you are getting at.

SOCRATES: What I am getting at is this: you do this wonderful feat of abstraction and you abstract sense observation and mathematical or logical reasoning from thinking in general and confine yourself to that and thus transform ordinary unscientific experience and thinking into scientific thinking. And there is nothing wrong with that. But then you forget the whole from which you have abstracted. You forget the richer, fuller thing from which you abstract these two very useful but narrow things. First you leave it behind, which is good, and then you forget it, which is bad, and then you deny it, which is very bad.

HUME: Be specific! What have I forgotten or denied?

SOCRATES: That humans do not merely think logically and scientifically, as animals cannot do, but also experience and feel and intuit and understand far more than animals do; that our reason understands far more than either an animal or a calculator does; that we possess not just a sensing mind and a calculating mind but much more.

HUME: You are now questioning my anthropology, not my method.

SOCRATES: That is correct. I have nothing against your method in science. But since philosophy is the love of wisdom rather than just the love of scientific knowledge, I question the adequacy of your method for philosophy, just as I questioned Descartes'. (Once again, as in our first conversation, you seem more in agreement with the Rationalist than in disagreement.)

HUME: But all the other sciences progressed when they began to use the scientific method. Why not philosophy?

SOCRATES: You sound *exactly* like Descartes now!

HUME: That is not a refutation or an answer to my question.

SOCRATES: No, but it is an illuminating comparison.

HUME: What is your answer to my question? Why shouldn't philosophy progress just as all the other sciences did when they used the scientific method?

SOCRATES: Because philosophy is not a science. Not in the modern sense, not in your sense. It is the love of *wisdom*. It seeks understanding, not just knowledge and facts.

HUME: Why must it be that? What justifies your kind of philosophy more than mine?

SOCRATES: To answer your question very directly, my philosophy is for human beings, but yours is for animals plus computers. You implicitly reduce man to an animal plus a computer.

HUME: So you are really questioning my implied anthropology.

SOCRATES: Yes. "Know thyself" and all that. I was big on that, remember? And I do not recognize myself in your anthropology of animal plus computer. I cannot see much of an identity between a human being and a Humean being.

HUME: You have not refuted me logically. You have simply repeated your bad pun.

SOCRATES: I have rejected the narrowness of your implied anthropology, and the skeptical conclusions that result from it.

HUME: But you have still not refuted my specific argument about causal reasoning that leads to that skeptical conclusion.

SOCRATES: I shall do so now. Would you not agree that there are two kinds of causal reasoning? First, reasoning "forward", so to speak, from a cause to its effect, and, secondly, reasoning "backwards" from an effect to its cause?

HUME: Yes.

SOCRATES: Yet all your examples are examples of the first kind, and none of the second.

HUME: So?

SOCRATES: It may be that your critique is correct concerning the one but not the other. It may be, as common sense maintains, that we cannot predict what effect will result from any given cause if we have not seen it, but that we *can* know something of the cause, even when unseen, if we see the effect.

HUME: I do not see that at all. If we had never seen objects hitting each other, like billiard balls, we could no more do the one kind of causal reasoning than the other. We could not predict what we had never seen: either that the struck ball would move after the striking ball hit it, or that the motion in the second ball could be traced back to motion in the first one.

SOCRATES: That may be true for billiard balls, but it does not seem to be true for other cases. I cannot know a priori that my teaching will cause learning in a student, for the student may simply refuse to learn, or fall asleep, or forget; but I can know, a priori, that if I have learned something new, I must have been taught, whether by nature or by a human teacher. And if I had never seen birds and eggs before, I could not predict that birds would lay eggs; but if I see an egg, I know that it has a cause, and that the cause must account for everything in the effect, and that therefore if the effect has life, the cause has life. So I can know a priori that eggs cannot come from rocks, but must come from something alive, though I do not yet know that that living thing is a bird rather than a mammal. If I see a foot, I cannot know that it will leave a footprint, but if I see a footprint, I can know that it was made by some kind of foot-shaped thing. Surely my reasoning backwards, from effects to causes, is more justifiable than reasoning forwards from cause to effect.

And surely the most common kind of traditional metaphysical reasoning is the "backwards" kind rather than the "forward" kind—especially the metaphysical arguments for the existence of God. They could not possibly reason from cause to effect but only from effect to cause. They could not use reasoning "forward" from cause to effect to prove God because God is not an effect and has no cause. And they could not reason "forward" from God as cause to His effects because no one but a fool pretends that he can predict what kind of universe God will create as His effect on the basis of knowing the nature of God, or the ideas of God, or the motives of God, as the cause.

HUME: But Rationalist metaphysicians like Spinoza pretend to do just that. They do philosophy and theology "in modo geometrico", by reasoning "forward", from cause to effect, as the geometricians do, deducing attributes from essences, like deducing that triangles have 180 degrees in their interior angles from the definition of a triangle, as Euclid does.

SOCRATES: And your critique of these Rationalist metaphysicians is quite valid, I think. But your critique does not touch of the other kind of metaphysics, the Aristotelian and Thomistic kind, who reason "backward".

HUME: I do not think you have proved your case, Socrates. You have only stated it. You have presented another account of causal reasoning but you have not proved your account, or disproved my account, or answered all my questions.

SOCRATES: What questions have I not answered?

HUME: The one in the next section, on causal connection.

SOCRATES: Then let us consider that next.

7

The Mysterious Idea
of Causal Connection

HUME: Here is my question, which you have not yet
answered, Socrates:

These two propositions are far from being E, IV
the same: *I have found that such an object* [for
instance, a bird, or a billiard ball hitting another]
has always been attended with such an effect
[for instance, an egg, or the second billiard ball
moving], and *I foresee that other objects, which
are in appearance, similar, will be attended with
similar effects.* I shall allow, if you please, that
the one proposition may justly be inferred
from the other: I know, in fact, that it always is inferred. But if you insist that the
inference is made by a chain of reasoning,
I desire you to produce that reasoning. The
connexion between these propositions is not
intuitive. There is required a medium, which
may enable the mind to draw such an inference, if indeed it be drawn by reasoning and
argument. What that medium is, I must con-
fess, passes my comprehension; and it is incumbent on those to produce it, who assert

**that it really exists, and is the origin of all
our conclusions concerning matter of fact.**

Please keep in mind this question of mine, Socrates—my demand that you produce this mysterious medium—as I proceed to explain further. I will expect a direct answer to this direct question.

Let me then repeat the principle of my previous chapter about the two kinds or categories of reason, so we can see which of these two categories your answer will fit into:

E, IV, 2   **All reasonings may be divided into two kinds,
namely demonstrative reasoning, or that concerning relations of ideas, and moral** [practical, probable] **reasoning, or that concerning
matter of fact and existence.**

SOCRATES: We have already explored this distinction, David: your sharp separation of reason from fact, your confinement of the objects of reason to mere ideas, and your reduction of all objective facts to material events that we can sense. Skepticism immediately follows, for we can no longer know by reason any matter of fact.

HUME: To call me a skeptic is not to refute me.

SOCRATES: It is if skepticism is self-contradictory. This skeptical philosophy of yours—is it objectively true? Is it a matter of fact? Or is it just a subjective idea, merely in your mind?

HUME: It is a matter of fact.

SOCRATES: Then according to your own principles, you cannot reach it by reasoning, but only by sense observation. But you do reach it by the long process of reasoning in your book, and not by sense observation. For of course you *cannot* reach it by sense observation, for skepticism is an idea, not a fact like the sunrise. It does not register on the senses. So your principle here, your separation of reason from facts, your distinction between "relations of ideas" and "matters of fact", contradicts itself.

HUME: We have gone over that argument of yours already, Socrates.

SOCRATES: And you have not yet refuted it.

HUME: Let me finish *my* argument first, please, before we argue about your refutation of it.

SOCRATES: Fine. Proceed.

HUME: Since there are no demonstrative arguments in the case of the billiard balls, or the sunrise it seems evident, since it implies no contradiction to believe that the second ball will not move when struck by the first, or that the sun will not rise tomorrow, that the course of nature may change, and that an object seemingly like those which we have experienced may be attended with different or contrary effects.

We cannot be sure that birds will not lay stones tomorrow instead of eggs, or that water may run uphill instead of down, for "the uniformity of nature" is assumed but not proved. If gravity became antigravity tomorrow, water would begin to run uphill instead of down.

You see, this *assumption* about the uniformity of nature undercuts all our claims to certainty, for it is an assumption that cannot be proved. As I say in the next paragraph,

E, IV, 2   **We have said [1] that all arguments concerning existence are founded on the relation of cause and effect; [2] that our knowledge of that relation is derived entirely from experience; and [3] that all our experimental conclusions proceed upon the supposition that the future will be conformable to the past** ["the uniformity of nature"]. **To endeavour, therefore, the proof of this last supposition by probable arguments, or arguments regarding existence** ["matters of fact"], **must be evidently going in a circle, and taking that for granted, which is the very point in question.**

SOCRATES: You have indeed proved that we cannot prove the general uniformity of nature from the premise of observed uniformities in fact. I think your proof is valid. For as you say, **"all inferences from experience suppose, as their foundation, that the future will resemble the past, and that similar powers will be conjoined with similar sensible qualities."** You cannot prove the uniformity of nature by arguments from experience, for all arguments from experience *presuppose* the uniformity of nature.

E, IV, 2

Incidentally, you later use this same principle, that of the uniformity of nature, in your proof that miracles never happen. There, you will affirm the principle as a certain premise; but, here, you deny that it is certain. But we should probably not get into that now, but wait until we take up the topic of miracles later.

HUME: What I want to do now is to prove that we cannot know matters of fact in the world by Descartes' rationalistic method of "clear and distinct ideas" alone, without experience . . .

SOCRATES: If you will permit me to interrupt, I think this proof too will be quite valid. It is the point I quoted from Chesterton a little while ago. Go on, then.

HUME:

> May I not clearly and distinctly conceive that   E, IV, 2
> a body, falling from the clouds, and which in
> all other respects resembles snow, has yet the
> taste of salt or [the] feeling of fire? Is there
> any more intelligible proposition than to af-
> firm, that all the trees will flourish in De-
> cember and January, and decay in May and
> June? Now whatever is intelligible, and can
> be distinctly conceived, implies no contra-
> diction, and can [therefore] never be proved
> false by any demonstrative argument or ab-
> stract reasoning *a priori.*
> If we be, therefore, engaged by arguments
> to put trust in past experience, and make it
> the standard of our future judgement, these
> arguments must be probable only. . . .

SOCRATES: I appreciate your habit of asking direct, clear, challenging questions, David, especially the one about the medium, the middle term or middle premise between "all men have died" and "I will die", or between "the sun has risen" and "it will rise tomorrow."

HUME: And I will appreciate your direct, clear answer to that question if you have one. I have not heard one yet.

SOCRATES: I do have one; and it comes from my intellectual grandson Aristotle, the father of inductive metaphysics, or a posteriori metaphysics, or metaphysics based on experience, rather than from my intellectual son Plato, the father of deductive metaphysics, or a priori metaphysics, or metaphysics based on pure reason. It is, in a word, *the abstraction of universal principles from the particulars known by sense experience.* The "medium" you sought is *universals*, or essences. That is the metaphysical side of the answer. But of course your Nominalism leaves no room for univerals. Or for metaphysics.

HUME: I am suspicious of metaphysics because I am suspicious of the rationalistic epistemology that underlies it. How do you know these "essences"? Certainly not by sense observation. I see horses but not horseness.

SOCRATES: We find universals by abstraction. That is the epistemological side of the answer.

HUME: And that is what I am suspicious of: airy abstractions that are like clouds, or birds flying through the air with no resistance. Empirical statements stay on the ground, like animals, and there can be resistance to them. A deer must be careful not to run into trees. But there are no trees in the sky. An Empiricist like myself must be careful not to be refuted by facts. Our claims are refutable in principle, by facts, by sense observation. And that is why empirical science progresses: because false hypotheses can be proved false by observation of matters of fact. But metaphysics is only about relations of ideas, and that is why its hypotheses cannot be proved false, unless they are self-contradictory. And that is why there has been no progress in metaphysics. Leibniz and Locke argued about many of the same issues that Plato and Aristotle argued about. And those arguments will go on forever, because they will never be refuted by facts, as empirical statements can be, because there are no facts in metaphysics. And there are no facts there because there is nothing we can sense there. We do not sense abstractions.

Now if you can convince me that we have some knowledge of matters of fact beyond what we have sensed, I will listen. But I very much doubt you will find any, not even one single example of it. I challenge you: give me one example of a matter of fact that we can know to be true with certainty even though we have not sensed it.

SOCRATES: That is not difficult. I have given you one such example already. You know that you will die. Do you doubt that?

HUME: No.

SOCRATES: But how do you know it?

HUME: By my sense observation of the fact that all men die, of course.

SOCRATES: No, that does not give you certainty, only probability.

HUME: But that is all I have in this case. It is extremely probable that I will die, just as it is extremely probable that the sun will rise.

SOCRATES: No, the two cases are not the same.

HUME: Why not? How are they different?

SOCRATES: We cannot know with certainty that the sun will rise tomorrow merely because we have sensed the sun rising every morning: you are right there. The fact that the sun has risen every morning does not prove it will rise tomorrow. But I can go further than sense observation in two different ways: one way in the case of the sun and another way in the case of my own death.

HUME: I would like to hear these two ways explained.

SOCRATES: Nothing is easier. First, the case of the sun rising. I agree with you that we cannot be absolutely certain that the sun will rise tomorrow, but I believe we can do more than merely observe that it has risen every day and conclude that it is very, very probable that it will go on doing it tomorrow.

HUME: We can do more than that because of the uniformity of nature?

SOCRATES: No, quite apart from that.

HUME: Then how?

SOCRATES: Because I can do more than sensing and remembering my sense observations. Animals can do that too. But I can do some things with my mind that animals cannot do, and one of these is that I can also *understand the cause*, the real reason, the principle, the explanation for the effect that I see; and then, if that understanding is valid, I can not only predict that I will see it again as a matter of fact, but also *understand the reason*. And I can understand that the reason is either contingent and changeable, as is the case with the sun, or necessary and unchangeable and essential, as is the case with my own death.

HUME: I do not understand either case, or the difference between the two. Explain how you come to this understanding.

SOCRATES: It's very simple, and you know it as well as I do. We can understand that the sun rises *because* the earth rotates, and thus as long as the earth rotates and the sun remains, the sun will rise. Perhaps I cannot know that the earth will not stop rotating, so I cannot know with certainty that the sun will rise tomorrow. Indeed, the earth may fly off its orbit into the darkness of outer space and freeze, due to some previously unknown force, in which case the sun will not rise tomorrow, or ever again. Or the sun may not remain, but explode into a supernova tonight and burn up the earth in an instant, and in that case it will *not* rise tomorrow, or any other day.

HUME: So you still cannot be certain that the sun will rise tomorrow.

SOCRATES: No, but I can go beyond sensation and probability: I can give the *reason why* it is so probable.

HUME: I see. I admit that we can do that, though not with certainty.

SOCRATES: So we agree in the case of the sun. But we do not agree in the case of my death. For I think I know that my mortality is not only highly probable, but certain.

HUME: How?

SOCRATES: Because I can know that all men are mortal, and I am a man, therefore I must be mortal.

HUME: Well, of course that syllogism is valid, but how do you know the major premise, that all men are mortal?

SOCRATES: In the same way I explained before. I can know that all men are mortal because I can know that all men have organic bodies—without a body, one may be a ghost or a god or an angel, but not a man—and I can know that organic bodies are by nature mortal since the organs can always stop working and cooperating. Those two premises justify my conclusion that all men are mortal. They also, by the way, give the reason why it is so, just as in the case of the sunrise.

HUME: Are you claiming that you can bypass sense observation? That these are "relations of ideas"?

SOCRATES: No. They are neither mere sense observations nor mere relations of ideas. They escape your two little categories.

HUME: So you deny that all learning depends on sense experience.

SOCRATES: I do not deny that. I affirm it. I agree that I cannot know these universal principles without any sense experience to begin with.

HUME: So you do not have an innate idea of man or mortality or sunrise a priori, before sense observation.

SOCRATES: Indeed not.

HUME: Then are you saying that you can deduce them from other a priori ideas without any sense experience?

SOCRATES: No, I am not.

HUME: You seem to have changed your mind since you met me. In Greece, you believed in innate ideas.

SOCRATES: It was Aristotle who changed my mind, not you. As Plato pictured me in some of his early dialogues, I did believe in that theory of innate ideas, but I no longer believe it. Aristotle convinced me that I was wrong. That is why I am now defending his epistemology rather than what you probably think of as Socratic and Platonic epistemology.

HUME: I see. But you still did not explain how you move from the sense experience that you say you need to start with, to the universal principles that you say you end with.

SOCRATES: That is where abstraction comes in. Once I have the experience—of man and mortality, for instance—I can also abstract the essentials, which are necessary and universal, from the accidents, which are contingent and particular. For instance, I can distinguish accidental causes of death, like drowning, from essential causes of death, the heart and brain stopping. And I can know that this is a universal possibility for all men because their bodies are organisms, and an organism dies if its organs stop cooperating. So I know not only the fact but the reason, and the essential and necessary nature of the reason.

Then, from the knowledge of this universal essence called humanity, which includes a body, and organs, and a heart and a brain and the dependence of the whole organism on the organs working and cooperating, I can deduce what follows from it: I can deduce mortality from humanity—not as a mere "relation of ideas" but because I *understand* humanity.

That is the medium you ask for, the thing you forget, or deny, or leave out of your epistemology. Your human knower is merely an ape plus a computer: senses, which tell you what but not why, facts but not reasons, and the mind, which merely knows the logical relationships between ideas, whether any two ideas are contradictory or not. Surely we can do, and do do, far more than those two things.

HUME: So you say we can understand the essences of things.

SOCRATES: Yes! For the essences of things are simply the natures of things. If you cannot know the essence of things, you cannot know *what* anything is, not even what an apple is. Surely you know what an apple is, David? If not, please do not invite me to your house to eat.

HUME: I am suspicious of all talk about "essences".

SOCRATES: I know. You are a Nominalist. You deny the existence of universals. That is your problem.

HUME: Why is it a problem?

SOCRATES: Because it leads to skepticism, as we have seen.

HUME: And why is *that* a problem?

SOCRATES: Because skepticism is self-contradictory, as we have also seen.

HUME: Ah, simple skepticism is. But not moderate or mitigated skepticism. And that is what I hold.

SOCRATES: Does this mean that you have an explanation for causal reasoning? That you have an answer to your own question about the "medium"? For you do not accept Aristotle's answer, so either you have no answer, and are a simple skeptic, or you have another one.

HUME: Indeed I do have another one. The "medium" is custom.

SOCRATES: Since that is in your next section, let us examine it next.

HUME: Wait! You have not fairly looked at my critique of causal connection yet. I thought that was the topic we were supposed to be discussing in this conversation.

SOCRATES: Then please state this critique for me.

HUME: Thank you. I say that since ideas are copies of impressions,

E, VII,
I

To be fully acquainted, therefore, with the idea of power or necessary [causal] connexion, let us examine its impression; and in order to find the impression with greater certainty, let us search for it in all the sources, from which it may possibly be derived.

When we look about us towards external objects, and consider the operation of causes, we are never able, in a single instance, to discover any power or necessary connexion; any quality, which binds the effect to the cause, and renders the one an infallible consequence of the other. We only find that the one does actually, in fact, follow [from] the other. The impulse of one billiard-ball is attended with motion in the second. This is the whole that appears to the *outward* senses. [And] the mind feels no sentiment or *inward* impression from this succession of objects: Consequently, there is not, in any single particular instance of cause and effect, anything which can suggest the idea of power or necessary connexion. . . .

E, VII,
I

Since, therefore, external objects as they appear to the senses, give us no idea of power or necessary connexion . . . let us see, whether this idea be derived from reflection on the operation of our own minds. . . .

It may be said, that we are every moment conscious of internal power; while we feel, that, by the simple command of our will, we can move the organs of our body, or direct the faculties of our mind. An act of volition produces motion in our limbs, or raises a new

idea in our imagination. This influence of
the will we know by consciousness. Hence
we acquire the idea of power or energy. . . .
[T]he motion of our body follows upon the
command of our will. Of this we are every
moment conscious. But the means, by which
this is effected; the energy, by which the will
performs so extraordinary an operation; of
this we are so far from being immediately
conscious that it must for ever escape our
most diligent enquiry.

For . . . is there any principle in all nature more mysterious than the union of soul
with body; by which a supposed spiritual substance acquires such an influence over a material one, that the most refined thought is
able to actuate the grossest matter? Were
we empowered, by a secret wish, to remove
mountains, or control the planets in their
orbit; this extensive authority would not be
more extraordinary nor more beyond our
comprehension. . . .

We learn the influence of our will from experience alone. And experience only teaches
us, how one event constantly follows another,
without instructing us in the secret connexion which binds them together, and renders
them inseparable.

SOCRATES: Here you seem to say two things: first,
that we do not *know* this causal connection, or necessity, or power because we do not *see* it, and, second, that the source of the idea is our own experience of our own will apparently causing our limbs to

E, VII,
I

move. The second idea seems quite reasonable to me, but the first one simply depends on your Empiricist premise again: we do not know it because we do not see it. So that is nothing new; it is just another consequence logically deduced from your first premise. And the deduction seems quite logical. So I have no complaints, except about your Empiricist premise.

HUME: I am surprised to hear that. I thought you specialized in complaints.

SOCRATES: Only when I find something to complain about. So I suppose it is now time to explore your positive answer to the question of the "medium" that justifies causal reasoning. If it is not what the masses think, what is it? What is the cause of causal reasoning?

HUME: In one word, it is custom.

SOCRATES: Then to the custom house we must go.

HUME: If I continue to find there such bad puns as that, I will complain as much as you do.

SOCRATES: Good arguments and bad puns—not a bad combination for a philosopher, I think.

HUME: Do you think good arguments justify bad puns?

SOCRATES: No. No more than better puns justify worse arguments.

8

Hume's Explanation of Causal Reasoning by Custom or Habit

SOCRATES: Here is what you say in Section V about the psychological connection, in our own minds, between our knowledge of the cause and our knowledge of the effect. It is not learning, or understanding, or abstraction, all of which are intellectual activities, but only custom, which is not an act of the intellect at all, but something we share with the animals.

> [H]e has not, by all his experience, acquired any idea or knowledge of the secret power [of causality] **by which the one object produces** [causes] **the other; nor is it, by any process of reasoning,** [that] **he is engaged to draw this inference. But still he finds himself determined to draw it: And though he should be convinced that his understanding has no part in the operation, he would nevertheless continue in the same course of thinking. There is some other principle which determines him to form such a conclusion.**
>
> **This principle is** *Custom* **or** *Habit*. **For wherever the repetition of any particular act or operation produces a propensity to renew**

E, V, 1

the same act or operation, without being impelled by any reasoning or process of the understanding, we always say, that this propensity is the effect of *Custom*. By employing
that word, we pretend not to have given the
ultimate reason of such a propensity. We
only point out a principle of human nature,
which is universally acknowledged, and which
is well known by its effects. . . . After the
constant conjunction of two objects — heat
and flame . . . we are determined by custom
alone to expect the one from the appearance
of the other. This hypothesis seems even the
only one which explains the difficulty, why
we draw, from a thousand instances, an inference which we are not able to draw from one
instance, that is, in no respect, different from
them. Reason is incapable of any such variation. The conclusions which it draws from
considering one circle are the same which it
would form upon surveying all the circles in
the universe. But no man, having seen only
one body move after being impelled by another, could infer that every other body will
move after a like impulse. All inferences from
experience, therefore, are effects of custom,
not of reasoning.

E, V, 1   Having found in many instances that any
two kinds of objects, flame and heat, snow
and cold — have always been conjoined together, if flame or snow be presented anew
to the senses, the mind is carried by cus-

tom to expect heat or cold. . . . It is an operation of the soul, when we are so situated,
as unavoidable as to feel the passion of love,
when we receive benefits; or hatred, when we
meet with injuries. All these operations are
a species of natural instincts, which no reasoning or process of the thought and understanding is able either to produce or to pre-
vent.

SOCRATES: I have four questions about your explanation, David.

My first question is this: You say that we cannot
know causality as we usually think we know it, namely
as an objective reality, as some physical force or energy that flows from one event to another. Is that
right?

HUME: Yes. For our sensory experience is our only
channel of knowledge of objective reality, and no
matter how hard we strain our eyes, we can never
see causality. We only see events, not the so-called
causal relation between events.

SOCRATES: So you explain *why we explain* things in
terms of causality instead of explaining any real, objective causal relationship between events. You explain the subjective causality between custom or habit
and our causal explanations, rather than the objective
causality between two real events.

HUME: That is exactly what I explain.

SOCRATES: And this is purely psychological, or subjective.

HUME: Yes, but it is present in all individuals. It does not distinguish one person from another. All of us think in this way.

SOCRATES: Because of common custom, or habit.

HUME: Yes.

SOCRATES: So you say it is not because of real causality, or because of our knowledge of real causality, that we use this category.

HUME: Yes, yes. Why do you repeat my point?

SOCRATES: Because I want to be sure I have your point clear before I point out to you that you seem to contradict yourself.

HUME: What? Where?

SOCRATES: First, you say that custom, or instinct, or habit, is the "cause" of our explaining things by causality. You explain this propensity of ours as the *real effect* of habit, as *really caused by* habit. So causality is real after all, though it is psychological rather than physical.

HUME: No, it is only a custom, whether it is used to explain physical events or mental events.

SOCRATES: *All* our knowledge of causality is only custom?

HUME: Yes.

SOCRATES: Then the relation between that custom or habit and its effect, which is our causal explanations, is itself only a custom, and not a relation of real causality. So you cannot say that our propensity to

explain events by causes is really caused by anything
real at all! How could a real propensity be caused by
a cause that is not real? How could there be more
reality in the effect than in the cause?

You see, if causality is only psychological custom or
habit, it cannot be known to be objectively real but
only subjective and psychological, then you cannot
say that custom *really* causes us to expect similar effects from similar causes. If all causality is only mental, and not real, mental causality is also only mental
and not real. So custom doesn't really cause or explain anything at all!

HUME: I will have to think that logical problem
through. There does seem to be a self-contradiction
there.

SOCRATES: My second question is this: you are a
Nominalist, are you not?

HUME: Yes.

SOCRATES: And you deny that universals are objectively real, isn't that right?

HUME: Yes. What is universal is words, names, *nom-
ina*. We use a common name like "tree" to refer
to many different things that resemble each other
closely enough so that we use the same word for all
of them.

SOCRATES: But you seem to abandon your Nominalism in the passage I quoted above from your book
where you say that we reason causally only within
a "kind" or species. We see one bird lay one egg,
and we expect other birds to lay other eggs. That

presupposes that we know that a bird is one kind of creature, different from a flower, and that an egg is different from a stone. We see the sun rise on many days in the past, so we expect the sun to rise every day, including tomorrow. But this presupposes that we know what a day is, and what a morning is, and what a sunrise is. We think in kinds, or species. But kinds or species are universals, not individuals. So we do know universal or general ideas or species after all.

HUME: We do not. I shall have to revise my wording and be more careful not to imply anything incompatible with Nominalism.

SOCRATES: I look forward to your revision. But I predict that it will be unreadable.

HUME: Why?

SOCRATES: I see no way of speaking about anything without using universals, unless you are simply calling people or animals each by its proper name, like "Here, Fido!" and "Here, Lassie!" But even then, "here" functions as a universal . . .

HUME: Of course *words* are universal. I admit that. It is a kind of shorthand.

SOCRATES: But you say that the things these universal words refer to are not objectively real.

HUME: That is what I say.

SOCRATES: But if the things the words refer to are not real, outside the words themselves, then the words cannot be *true*. For what else do we mean by true words if not words that refer to real things?

For instance, the words "The sky is blue" are true if and only if the real sky really is really blue.

HUME: I cannot deny that that is what everyone means by truth.

SOCRATES: And here is a third problem I have with that passage that I just quoted. As you did before, so here again you again reduce reason to reasoning, understanding to proving, intellectual intuition to demonstration, what traditional logic calls the "first act of the mind" to "the third act of the mind".

HUME: And what is that "first act of the mind"?

SOCRATES: The comprehension of the meaning of a concept or an essence or a "what" or a kind—the thing Nominalists deny. For instance, do you know what an healthy apple is and what a poisonous mushroom is?

HUME: If I say I do, then I say I know a "what", a universal essence, and you will say that I have abandoned Nominalism. So I will not abandon Nominalism. So what do you say to that?

SOCRATES: I say here, as I said earlier, please do not ever invite me to eat at your house. For if you do not know what a healthy apple is or what a poisonous mushroom is, then you may well feed me a poisonous mushroom, mistaking it for a healthy apple.

HUME: You have substituted a culinary refutation for a logical one, Socrates.

SOCRATES: No, because my refutation is intellectually delicious, not physically delicious. My question is about your answer to your question in your third paragraph. There, you say that it is two things that cause us to think that one of the two causes the other. But two people observe the same constant conjunction and yet one sees a causal connection sooner than the other. After seeing a few people die, the wise understand the reason for death, as I explained before, and the necessity of it, while the less wise do not. What causes this difference? My epistemology answers that question: the wise understand essences and essential causal connections more quickly and clearly than the unwise. You cannot use that explanation, because you deny essences, essential causal connections, understanding, and wisdom. So I wonder how your epistemology could account for this innate difference in wisdom between two people.

HUME: I deny it. I am an egalitarian.

SOCRATES: Exactly like Descartes at the beginning of his *Discourse on Method*.

HUME: An accusation of "guilt by association" is not an argument.

SOCRATES: Nor is the accusation of that accusation an answer. But I also have a fourth quarrel with your passage, in that your explanation seems to confuse the three distinct meanings of the word "because", namely, (1) the relation between a premise and a conclusion, (2) the relation between a physical cause and an effect, and (3) the relation between a subjective motive for acting and a human action, whether the action is mental or physical. You confuse the logical "because", the physical "because", and the psychological "because".

Thus we say that x = 2 *because* x = one quarter of

y and y = 8; or we say that whales are mammals *be-cause* any animal that has warm blood and gives birth to live offspring are mammals and whales are animals that have warm blood and give birth to live offspring. That is the logical "because", the "because" that indicates a reason or premise, a piece of proof or evidence, a reason for believing the conclusion.

We also say that the street is wet *because* it rained, or that a man died *because* he ate one of your poisoned mushrooms. (Isn't that how Buddha died? Was it one of your disciples that fed him that meal, David? Did your Nominalism do him in, poor fellow?) This is the physical cause, and the relation between physical cause and effect, the relation you have so devastatingly criticized.

Finally, we also say that "He is depressed *because* he was just fired" or "He believes in God *because* he is afraid to die" or "He is an atheist *because* he is too proud to admit his inferiority." This is the psychological "because". These are psychological explanations.

Now *you* seem to reduce the other two kinds of "becauses" to psychological "becauses". And this seems to mean that you are reducing all sciences to psychology. Physics, astronomy, biology, and all other sciences that have always believed they were explaining the real physical world by their causal explanations—these were all deluded, if you are right, and all scientists should resign in shame or become psychologists.

HUME: Those are four large quarrels, Socrates. May I have your permission to think about them for a while before I try to answer them?

SOCRATES: Not only my permission but my blessing. In fact, you do not have my permission *not* to think about them before you try to answer them. For that would be thoughtless rather than rational. That would be speaking by instinct, or custom, or habit, or some such insultingly subrational way of speaking. And I would certainly not expect you to fall to that low level, since you are such a clever reasoner.

HUME: In other words, you expect me not to practice the irrational philosophy I preach. Is that it?

SOCRATES: I couldn't have put the point any better than that myself.

9

Hume's Emotive Morality

SOCRATES: The next subject I want to investigate is not covered in the book we are investigating, the *Enquiry concerning Human Understanding*.

HUME: Then why cover it here?

SOCRATES: Because it is the single most important idea in your entire philosophy, it seems to me, because it makes the greatest difference to human life.

HUME: And why is that?

SOCRATES: It is what philosophers have called "the emotive theory of morality", which is essentially your reduction of objectively real moral good and evil to subjective feeling and emotion.

HUME: So since this idea is so important, you do not want to ignore it.

SOCRATES: Yes. And a second justification for bringing it in here is that the premises or foundations of this "most important idea" of yours are the ones we have already considered, so that this "most important idea" of yours is a logical corollary of the ideas we have already discussed.

HUME: Feel free to investigate it, then.

SOCRATES: And a third justification for speaking of this moral idea of yours is that it is so similar to the idea of causality that we have just discussed. With regard to morality, just as in regard to causality, you reduce something that most people believe to be objective to something purely subjective.

HUME: On the other hand, since your investigation is supposed to deal only with my one little book on epistemology, we should not take up much time investigating this other idea of mine, nor quote extensively from my other books and carefully analyze the wording of their arguments, as you have done for my epistemology.

SOCRATES: I agree. I will only investigate three things about your moral philosophy: your essential premise, your essential conclusion, and the essential corollary in practice that follows from your theoretical conclusion. So I shall quickly summarize these three points of your moral philosophy, and ask you whether I have misunderstood it in any way. Is that all right with you?

HUME: Apparently you are the one who sets up the rules here, Socrates, so please proceed.

SOCRATES: Appearances are deceiving. I am merely the servant of the One who sets up the rules here.

HUME: Ah, yes, I see . . . uh . . . could we defer that subject until later, preferably much later?

SOCRATES: I had not planned to enter that area. That is for one far more wise than I. I am merely a philosopher, and this is merely your intellectual Purgatory.

HUME: So I will not have to defend my agnosticism to you.

SOCRATES: Not unless it is part of your book.

HUME: Oh. I thought you were going to go into God-talk now.

SOCRATES: I hadn't intended to. I merely mentioned Him in correcting your mistake about my role here.

HUME: Fine. Let us proceed.

SOCRATES: I see your epistemology as your foundation for every other part of your philosophy. And your epistemology is essentially Empiricism. That is the reason for your critique of causality, for instance: that sense experience is our only channel of access to the real world, and sense experience never is an experience of the causal relation itself but only an experience of the two events. That is also the reason for your Nominalism, for sense experience never is an experience of the universal, but only of the individual, the particular.

HUME: You are correct so far, Socrates.

SOCRATES: So with Empiricism as your premise, you cannot admit the knowledge of a real moral law, or moral obligations, or moral rights, or moral duties, or moral goods, or moral evils, virtues and vices, for all these things are nonempirical. They cannot be seen, and they have no color or size or shape.

HUME: I do not deny the reality or importance of these moral things, Socrates. I just deny that they form part of the furniture of Heaven and earth, part of objective reality. They are part of the furniture of the human mind, or the human soul. And there, they are very important. I believe that morality is *subjective*, but I do not conclude that it is *unimportant*. If the unimportance of morality is supposed to be the corollary you were about to deduce from my main point of the subjectivity of morality, I do *not* agree.

SOCRATES: But the unimportance of morality is the corollary that most people would deduce from your main principle that morality is subjective. For it does seem that if morality is not objectively real but only subjective, only psychological, then we will not take it as seriously, just as we take an imagined lion, or an imagined fortune, less seriously than a real one.

HUME: That is the corollary that I deny.

SOCRATES: But before we get to the corollary, let us be sure we understand the principle. Just what do you mean by saying that morality is subjective?

HUME: Those are not the words I use, but I will let you use them. But I would rather simply try to summarize my view of the ontological status of morality for you, Socrates, in a very simple and popular way.

SOCRATES: Be my guest.

HUME: Remember that our sense experience is our only direct channel to the real world. Now suppose you see an event that provokes you to make a moral judgment—let us say that you see a frail little old lady being assaulted and robbed on a dark city street by a strong young man with a weapon. He hits her on the head with a club. She falls bleeding to the street. He runs away with her purse. And you have seen all these events. And when you see them, three things happen inside you. First, your feelings change. You were happy and at peace, but now you are angry and upset. Second, you also make a moral judgment, a judgment of moral value: you say that that deed of robbery was an evil deed, an immoral deed, and that the robber is an evil and immoral man. And, third, you try to undo the deed, as far as you can: you try to help the victim, or catch the robber, or both. Your feelings and your judgment move you to action.

SOCRATES: No one would quarrel with your scenario so far.

HUME: But here is my question, and many *will* quarrel with my answer to it. Just *where* is the evil? Do we see it? Is it part of the universe? Is it in the robber, or the weapon, or the deed? Most people would say so. But it must be a *good* stroke of the club, and a *good* club, and a *good*, healthy arm to strike. And the blood that flows from the poor victim is good blood. Where is the evil? We cannot find it by looking for it. And that means that we cannot find it in the objective world. For you must remember my empirical premise: that our only channel to the objective world is sensation. My moral conclusion flows directly from that epistemological premise.

SOCRATES: Your moral conclusion seems more radical than your epistemological premise, but it does seem to logically follow. So perhaps your premise is also more radical than it seems.

HUME: I prefer to think that my conclusion is less radical than it seems, and more commonsensical. I think everyone can see how reasonable it is. For good and evil are not like square and round, or green and red: they are not sensed or sensible, ever, in principle. So they are not part of the objective world. And if they are not part of the objective world, then either they are utterly unreal and part of no world whatever, or else they are part of the subjective world, that rich world of our own thoughts, feelings, and experiencings. And that is what I maintain. We project our own bad feelings onto the man and the deed and call them "bad". It is not a moral mistake to do that—you are not wicked if you do that—but it is a philosophical mistake. You are naïve and mistaken when you do that without knowing you do it. You do not realize that when you judge that the robber is bad or that his act is bad, you are projecting your feelings out onto the objective world. That is what you have called "the emotive theory of morality".

SOCRATES: I understand. But surely the corollary follows then: if morality is only projected private feelings and not public facts, we will not take it seriously. For we have no obligation to our own feelings.

HUME: I do not agree that this corollary follows. For the subjective world is not less important than the objective world, but more important, since man is more important than the universe. Thus my transfer of moral reality from the objective world to the subjective world does not make morality less important but more so.

SOCRATES: But it is not just a matter of where morality lives, but where it comes from. When you say that it is "subjective", you mean not just "present in the world of subjectivity, the world of human consciousness", but "*originating* there". Morality for you is not a call from the real world that impinges upon our will and binds our will with a force that is real but not physical or even emotional or psychological, but moral. It is not a force that morally binds our will under moral obligation. Rather, morality for you is only our own subconscious projection, our own invention, like art, or the rules of a game. If we made the rules, why can't we change them? Why should we take them seriously if they come from us rather than to us? You seem to be like the man in the cartoon on the desert island. . . .

HUME: What cartoon is that?

SOCRATES: Two starving, shipwrecked men share a tiny desert island. One day a bottle washes ashore with a message in it. The first man picks it up, with hope in his eyes: it seems to be a message from the outside world. But when he reads it, his face falls, and he explains to the other man: "It's only from ourselves".

That is the difference between your theory of morality and that of the masses, it seems. They believe that the moral message in the bottle (let us call the bottle "conscience") came from outside, from objective reality—probably from God, ultimately. But you believe that "it's only from ourselves."

HUME: What else can I believe if I begin with my Empiricist premise and refuse to be illogical in drawing conclusions from it?

SOCRATES: Nothing, indeed. I rest my case.

HUME: You mean you claim to have refuted Empiricism as an epistemology by showing its moral consequences? A *reductio ad absurdum* argument?

SOCRATES: Exactly. The prosecution rests.

HUME: But where then do you say that morality comes from? Surely you do not want to go back to the "divine command theory" that you so nicely refuted in the "Euthyphro".

SOCRATES: No, but it is not my philosophy but yours that is under investigation now. And I think it is high time we returned to your book and investigated your famous critique of miracles.

10

Hume's Critique of Miracles

HUME: I have been much maligned concerning this topic. In the interest of fairness, I would like the privilege of summarizing my thoughts on it in my own way before you subject them to your critique, if that is all right with you.

SOCRATES: Certainly. But you must understand why people were so upset: the topic is not a peripheral one but a central and essential one in the Christian religion. Whether they are true or false, whether miracles really happen or not, nearly everything in Christianity is miraculous: the creation; the fall; the miracles, which are in both the Old Testament and the New; angels, prophecies; the Incarnation; Christ's divinity; His Resurrection; His Ascension; His Second Coming; man's new birth, resurrection, and glorification in Heaven—every one of those claims is a miraculous, supernatural event.

HUME: I am not a theologian. I do not claim to know how important miracles are. I am a philosopher, however, and I do claim to know how very, very unlikely miracles are, and how irrational it is to believe in them. May we hear my argument for that conclusion now?

SOCRATES: Indeed we may. After all, it is your book that we are investigating. Do you want to change anything you wrote in that book?

HUME: Indeed not. I stand by it.

SOCRATES: Then please summarize your argument against miracles. Arrange or rearrange it as you will, and add to it or explain it as you will, but please begin by quoting the salient points from Section X, "Of Miracles".

HUME: Gladly. I will do so in seven steps.

1. First, before applying my principles concerning what we should and should not believe to the issue of miracles, we need to state the principle. My first principle concerns the morality of belief. It is this: **A wise man proportions his belief to the evidence.**

E, X, 1

2. And since evidence comes from the experience of the senses, which discover events, variation in evidence comes from variation in experience. For

All effects follow not with like certainty from their supposed causes. Some events are found, in all countries and all ages, to have been constantly conjoined together. Others are found to have been more variable, and sometimes to disappoint our expectations; so that in our reasonings concerning matter of fact, there are all imaginable degrees of assurance. . . .

3. My next principle has been enunciated already, in the chapter on "necessary connection", but here I draw its consequences regarding whether how far we should believe human testimony. It is this:

It being a general maxim, that no objects
have any discoverable connexion together,
and that all the inferences, which we can
draw from one to another, are founded merely
on our experience of their constant and reg-
ular conjunction, it is evident that we ought
not to make an exception to this maxim in
favour of human testimony. . . .

And as the evidence derived from witnesses
and human testimony, is founded on past experience, so it varies with the experience,
and is regarded either as a *proof* or a *probability*, according as the conjunction between
any particular kind of report and any kind of
object has been found to be constant or variable.

4. I now define a miracle: **A miracle is a violation** E, X, 1
of the laws of nature. . . .

5. And I then apply my third principle to this definition of miracle, and come up with my main argument:

5A. **And as a firm and unalterable experience
has established these laws, the proof against
a miracle, from the very nature of the fact,
is as entire as any argument from experience
can possibly be imagined.**

5B. For

Nothing is esteemed a miracle, if it ever happen in the common course of nature. It is
no miracle that a man, seemingly in good
health, should die on a sudden; because such
a kind of death, though more unusual than

any other, has yet been frequently observed to happen. But it is a miracle, that a dead man should come to life; because that has never been observed in any age or country.

5c. So my conclusion against miracles seems a demonstrative proof:

There must, therefore, be a uniform experience against every miraculous event, otherwise the event would not merit that appellation. And as a uniform experience amounts to a proof, there is here a direct and full *proof*, from the nature of the fact, against the existence of any miracle.

6. Therefore, I draw this corollary:

E, X, 1   When anyone tells me, that he saw a dead man restored to life, I immediately consider with myself, whether it be more probable that this person should either deceive or be deceived, or that the fact which he relates should really have happened.

In other words, it is always more *probable* that a man is hallucinating or lying than that a miracle happen, since men often hallucinate or lie. Therefore, applying my first principle, that we ought to proportion our belief to evidence and probabilities, we should never believe in miracles.

7. Then, to bolster my main argument, I offer this further argument concerning the reliability of human testimony: that

there is not to be found, in all history, any E, X, 2
miracle attested by a sufficient number of
men, of such unquestioned good-sense, education, and learning as to secure us against
all delusion in themselves, of such undoubted
integrity as to place them beyond all suspicion of any design to deceive others; of such
credit and reputation in the eyes of mankind,
as to have a great deal to lose in case of their
being detected in any falsehood; and at the
same time, attesting facts performed in such
a public manner and in so celebrated a part
of the world, as to render the detection unavoidable.

SOCRATES: I am happy, David, that your training in
logic has enabled you to summarize your argument
so clearly and helpfully, so that all I have to do is
to explore each of your seven clearly distinguished
and clearly stated points, rather than to impose such
a clear logical order myself upon the disorderly reasoning of a less logical mind than yours.

HUME: Which less logical minds have you examined
here, Socrates?

SOCRATES: I have examined thinkers whose names
you would not recognize who came after you in history, when thinking logically will no longer be regarded as a virtue, thinkers with names like Marx,
Nietzsche, and Sartre. But we may not be distracted
by this. Back to our topic: miracles. You do not believe they ever happen, do you?

HUME: No. But that does not mean I do not believe in Christianity. I am a Christian, but a liberal Christian in my theology.

SOCRATES: I wonder why you call the denial of miracles "liberal".

HUME: Because everyone does. That is the common term.

SOCRATES: Then I wonder why everyone does, or why anyone does.

HUME: Because "liberal" means "free", and we liberals are freethinkers. We choose for ourselves which dogmas to believe and which to disbelieve among the dogmas of the old Christianity, or the conservative Christianity, or the orthodox Christianity. Why are you surprised at the term?

SOCRATES: Because of another passage I read in Chesterton. He wrote:

O, VIII   For some extraordinary reason, there is a fixed notion that it is more liberal to disbelieve in miracles than to believe in them. Why, I cannot imagine, nor can anybody tell me. . . .
     A holiday, like Liberalism, only means the liberty of man. A miracle only means the liberty of God. You may conscientiously deny either of them, but you cannot call your denial a triumph of the liberal idea. The Catholic Church believed that man and God both had a sort of spiritual freedom. Calvinism took away the freedom

from man, but left it to God. Scientific material-ism binds the Creator Himself; it chains up God as the Apocalypse chained the devil. It leaves nothing free in the universe. And those who as-sist this process are called the "liberal theolo-gians."

HUME: It is a question of terminology only, not of fact and substance.

SOCRATES: Perhaps. Perhaps not. We shall see more clearly only when we see your reasons more clearly.

HUME: Then let us consider them, beginning with my first point, that we ought to proportion our be-lief to the evidence.

SOCRATES: This principle will be called "Clifford's Rule", after a British logician. It would seem to be a good scientific principle, though not a good personal principle.

HUME: Why not? It excludes only prejudice.

SOCRATES: Yes, but prejudice may be a good thing.

HUME: What? I am shocked to hear you say that, Socrates.

SOCRATES: You disagree, then, that prejudice can ever be a good thing?

HUME: Indeed I do! Except perhaps in some extraor-dinary circumstance. But can you give me a common example of prejudice that you think it is a good thing?

SOCRATES: What about friendship? Do you think we should treat the stories and promises of our friends as we treat scientific hypotheses? Should we treat our friends as we treat chemicals in laboratories? Or should we make room for faith, for personal trust, for prejudice in favor of a friend?

HUME: Oh, well, of course we should trust our friends, if that's all you mean by "prejudice".

SOCRATES: I remember you were deeply disappointed in a former friend when you found out how untrustworthy he was. It was another philosopher.

HUME: Rousseau, you mean?

SOCRATES: Yes.

HUME: But when we are doing philosophy, at least we should confine ourselves to the impersonal and objective evidence, don't you agree?

SOCRATES: I think not.

HUME: Why not?

SOCRATES: Take the issue of miracles. You look at this as a philosophical issue, do you not?

HUME: I do.

SOCRATES: But what if some of the evidence for miracles is personal? What if all of it is personal?

HUME: Why do you think the evidence is personal?

SOCRATES: I have never heard of any laboratory evidence being claimed for miracles, have you?

HUME: Indeed not. That is why I do not believe them.

SOCRATES: But if they *could* be produced in laboratories, they would not be miracles, would they?

HUME: Indeed not. That is why I do not believe them.

SOCRATES: I see. You do not believe in miracles because they do not appear in laboratories. But if there were miracles, they would never appear in laboratories. Does that not seem like saying that you do not believe in birds because they never appear underground? But if there *were* birds, they would *never* appear underground. Your argument is circular.

HUME: I stand corrected on that argument. It is indeed circular. And I will accept your violation of Clifford's Rule when we are dealing with something personal. We should trust our friends, even beyond the scientific evidence. But I will not accept that concerning miracles. For miracles are not persons.

SOCRATES: But miracles (by definition, whether they really happen or not) are performed *by* persons, whether human or divine. And if God performs them, they are performed *for* human persons.

And they are *reported by* human persons, and they are *believed by* human persons. So the evidence for miracles has very much indeed to do with persons, and how much we may trust these persons.

HUME: I will acknowledge that. But I will also maintain that it is always more probable that persons are deceived or deceiving than that miracles happen. For there are many cases of deception, but few cases of miracles, even by the standards of the believer. That is the nub of my argument.

SOCRATES: But it seems you are once again eliminating the personal reckoning from the equation, for no good reason. When a person tells us that something happened, whether that something is miraculous or not, do we not size up the person, and how credible he is, before we decide to believe or disbelieve what he says?

HUME: Yes.

SOCRATES: So the personal element remains a part of our evidence. But what *you* mean by "evidence" seems to be merely the evidence of our senses.

HUME: Yes, that is what I do mean.

SOCRATES: But surely we have other kinds of evidence too, evidence of a person's character as more or less trustworthy. And surely we use that evidence when deciding whether or not to believe a person's testimony. And surely we assess that evidence—the evidence about a person's character—very differently, and with different powers of the mind, than we assess the evidence of our senses. We find it with other organs than our senses, and we judge it with other powers than our senses. For instance, when we buy a house or a car from that person, we judge the house in a purely empirical and scientific way, but we judge the person by other standards. And that is why I find your second point, about assessing *sensible* evidence, less than adequate as a principle of method when it comes to assessing *personal* evidence.

HUME: Then let us confine ourselves to assessing sensible evidence.

SOCRATES: But I do not even find your point adequate for assessing *sensible* evidence, for you say we should proportion our belief to frequency: the more often a thing happens, the more likely it is. But this is not always the case. Each baby has a new and different genetic code, but that does not make it unlikely. A car has started up every morning for ten thousand times in a row. That does not mean the starter will last forever and will not refuse to start tomorrow for the first time.

HUME: That is true, of course.

SOCRATES: So not only is Clifford's Rule not correct for assessing personal evidence, but proportioning our belief to frequency is not even correct for assessing sensible evidence.

HUME: Even if I acknowledge that, I do not see how that invalidates my subsequent argument.

SOCRATES: That is easy to see, if we state that argument in a syllogism. Its first premise is that we should proportion our belief to the evidence, and its second premise is that the evidence is a matter of frequency: the "constant cojoining together" versus the varying. That is the false premise. For each snowflake, and each fingerprint, and each human face, varies from every other one, and yet we do not disbelieve in the unique pattern of the next one. On the other hand, a person may lie habitually and constantly, but that does not mean we should believe him. It means that we should *not*.

HUME: The point is true but peripheral to my main argument against miracles.

SOCRATES: It is. So let us go to your third point. This point—that we do not *know* causal *connections* but only *observe* constant *conjunctions*—is the one you made earlier in your critique of causality. So I think we can pass over it also.

HUME: Why?

SOCRATES: Because I refuted that premise when I investigated your philosophy of causality.

HUME: Did you, really?

SOCRATES: Do you have an answer to my refutation now?

HUME: No . . .

SOCRATES: Then let us proceed to your fourth point, your definition of a miracle.

HUME: A miracle is a violation of some law of nature. Surely there is nothing wrong with that definition.

SOCRATES: Nothing except one thing: that it is not true.

HUME: What? Why?

SOCRATES: Take any example of a miracle. Pick one yourself.

HUME: A virgin birth.

SOCRATES: Good.

HUME: Surely that is a violation of a natural law.

SOCRATES: Only in one way: its cause was supernatural, not natural. But the effect is completely natural.

It takes nine months, and a womb, and blood, and food, and all the normal chemicals. It can die. (In fact, it does, thirty-three years later.)

HUME: Then take the Incarnation itself: the miracle of God becoming man, according to traditional Christian dogma.

SOCRATES: According to Christian dogma, Christ was completely man as well as completely God. He had to go to the bathroom every day. When he fasted, he got hungry. And, as I just mentioned, he could die and did, like any other man. You see, miracles are like meteors: once they enter the earth's atmosphere, they behave exactly like rocks that are native to this planet. They violate no laws of nature at all, but conform to them.

HUME: But they are still *caused* by an extraterrestrial cause.

SOCRATES: So you define a miracle as an event with a supernatural *cause*?

HUME: Yes.

SOCRATES: Then let us examine your definition. A definition has two parts, logically, does it not?—the genus and the specific difference?

HUME: Yes.

SOCRATES: And the genus in your definition of a miracle is—?

HUME: An event.

SOCRATES: And the specific difference?

HUME: Its cause is supernatural.

SOCRATES: Now in order to use any definition, we must understand it, must we not?

HUME: Of course.

SOCRATES: All parts of it, or only some?

HUME: All.

SOCRATES: Including the specific difference?

HUME: Yes.

SOCRATES: And the specific difference of your definition of miracle is—?

HUME: Its cause is supernatural.

SOCRATES: And having a supernatural cause is having a cause, of course.

HUME: Yes.

SOCRATES: But you say there is no knowledge of real causality.

HUME: There is not.

SOCRATES: Not for any man?

HUME: No.

SOCRATES: Are you a man?

HUME: Of course.

SOCRATES: Then you cannot know causality, or your own definition of miracle.

HUME: I will patch up that logical problem in future editions of my book.

SOCRATES: Alas, I fear there will be no time for any changes to your book.

HUME: Why?

SOCRATES: Haven't you heard the news? You can't go back to earth after death. There is no reincarnation. I was wrong in that guess of mine when I was in Greece.

HUME: You mean I am dead and not dreaming?

SOCRATES: You may be both, if there is dreaming after death, but yes, you are dead, and not just dreaming that you are dead.

HUME: Then I was as wrong about life after death as you were about reincarnation.

SOCRATES: Are you surprised to learn Lesson One?

HUME: Lesson One? What is Lesson One?

SOCRATES: How little we know. How often we err. What fools we mortals be.

HUME: Just get on with it, Socrates. Finish your autopsy on my book. It shouldn't take long. I'm glad I wrote such a short book.

SOCRATES: So were most of your readers.

HUME: So are the readers of most books. The popular ones are the short ones.

SOCRATES: Not all. That is not true of books that are deeply loved. For instance, lovers of Lewis Carroll would dearly love to have another Alice book. And Tolkien echoed the feelings of most of his readers when he said *The Lord of the Rings* was too short. (It was only about fifteen hundred pages.) But these are matters you know nothing about. Let us return to your book, which you do claim to know something about.

Your fifth point about miracles is your main argument. Let me summarize it again.

You say that the laws of nature are established by observation and induction, do you not?

HUME: Yes.

SOCRATES: And this establishes generalizations, about what happens always, or nearly always, as distinct from what does not. Isn't that true?

HUME: That's true.

SOCRATES: Now you say that a man rising from the dead would be a miracle because it is extremely rare; in fact, it has *never* happened before. But surely the reason why it would be a miracle that a dead man should rise is not simply because it has never happened before. Never before has anyone ever uttered the sentence "On June 12, 1334, two sick turkeys collided in mid air over Oslo, Norway." Yet there is nothing miraculous about that utterance—I just made it—or about the fact it claims. A miracle is *an event with a supernatural cause*, according to the definition of a miracle that we both agreed to. A miracle is not just a very unusual event but an event that could not have happened by natural causes, because they have not the power. That is why a man rising from the dead is a miracle. And that is the definition of a miracle that is used both by those who affirm them and by those who deny them.

Your next sentence, **"There must therefore be** E, X, 1
a uniform experience against every miraculous
event, otherwise the event would not merit that
appellation", seems a clear case of begging the question, deciding the issue simply be defining terms in
your way rather than in the common way. This argument does the same thing as Anselm's famous "ontological argument" for God. It gets its conclusion
simply out of its definition.

Further, you say that **"a uniform experience**
amounts to a proof." But it does not. In fact you
yourself admitted that it does not when you gave the
example of the sun rising every morning: this is a
uniform experience, but it does not prove it will rise
tomorrow. You were right there, and not here.

Finally, when you say it is always more probable
that those who claim to have seen miracles are lying
or hallucinating, how do you calculate how probable
it is that something new should happen that has never
happened before and thus qualify as a miracle and a
violation of a law of nature?

HUME: Only past observation can afford a ground for
future probabilities.

SOCRATES: But clearly we calculate future probabilities not merely by observation but by understanding
causes and casual powers. We know that it is more
probable that a man will write a kind of book that has
never been written before than that a man will father
a kind of child that has never been fathered before,
an immortal child, a god. We know this because we
understand that the man has the power to write a
new book but that he does not have the power to
father a new species, a god.

HUME: We differ about this, Socrates, because I trust only my senses, while you trust your power to intuit invisible metaphysical powers.

SOCRATES: Let's not argue about metaphysics here, but only about the logic of the argument, and the logic of probability. The nub of your argument against miracles, in one sentence, is this, is it not?—that it is always more probable that men are lying or hallucinating than that the miracles they claim to have seen really happened?

HUME: Yes. That is my main point.

SOCRATES: So it depends on probability.

HUME: Yes.

SOCRATES: The probability of statements about events that are said to occur in time, in history.

HUME: Yes.

SOCRATES: And what is the standard by which you judge how probable any such event is?

HUME: Frequency. How many times it is observed to have occurred.

SOCRATES: So sense observation is the standard of belief.

HUME: Yes. "Matters of fact", observed by the senses, are the standard for "relations of ideas", or beliefs. Objective facts are the standard. Surely you agree with that?

SOCRATES: I do, but I do not agree with your Empiricist assumption that the only way to know objective facts is by the senses alone. In any case, you say that the more often a thing has happened, the more probable it is that it will happen again.

HUME: Yes.

SOCRATES: And the less often, the less probable.

HUME: Yes.

SOCRATES: And the laws of nature are established with immense probability because they describe events that have been observed many, many times without exception?

HUME: Yes. They are supported by what I call "a firm and unalterable experience". Elsewhere I call it a "uniform experience". A universal experience.

SOCRATES: So there is uniform or universal experience against miracles.

HUME: Indeed. Otherwise it would not be called a "miracle".

SOCRATES: So a miracle is by definition the most improbable of all events.

HUME: Exactly. But people lying or hallucinating is never *that* improbable. Therefore if we apply Clifford's Rule and proportion our belief to the evidence, including the probability factor, we will never believe in a miracle. Because it is always more probable that the witnesses were deceived or deceiving than that a miracle happened.

SOCRATES: This seems to be a very strong argument indeed. For if its premise is true, if there is totally universal or uniform experience against miracles, then they are totally improbable.

HUME: So you agree.

SOCRATES: Almost.

HUME: But not quite? Somehow, I suspected you had an escape.

SOCRATES: I think I see just a little chink in your wall of "immense improbability" through which miracles might creep. Take this case. Let us say that it is almost totally improbable that one particular flea will find the one and only crack in a twenty-mile-long wall, the one crack that is just barely large enough for one flea to fly through in the few minutes during which the crack opens due to natural causes such as frost heaves, settling, or a slight earthquake, or some other natural event that damages the wall for only a few seconds and then instantly repairs it—perhaps it is one chance in a trillion trillion—but it is still *possible*. Do you want to say that miracles are just barely possible, one chance in a trillion trillion, let's say? Are they nearly infinitely improbable, but not quite infinitely improbable? Or do you want to say that they are infinitely improbable?

HUME: Infinitely improbable, since the experience of the uniformity of nature is not "nearly total" but total.

SOCRATES: So if even one miracle happened, this would refute the principle that nature is absolutely uniform.

HUME: Yes. For I say that miracles by definition contradict the laws of nature, which laws always presuppose the uniformity of nature.

SOCRATES: Let us leave aside my former point about the relation between miracles and the laws of nature: the point where I say the two do not contradict each other. Let us assume, as you say, that they do. Let us assume that the principle of the uniformity of nature excludes miracles.

HUME: Yes, let us assume that.

SOCRATES: *How do we know* this principle of the uniformity of nature?

HUME: By uniform, universal, total experience.

SOCRATES: Experience without exceptions.

HUME: Yes.

SOCRATES: But we know that this experience of the uniformity of nature, this experience of a miracleless nature, this experience against miracles—we know that this is true only if no miracles ever happen *and we know* that no miracles ever happen, only if all reports of miracles are false *and we know that* all reports of miracles are false.

HUME: Yes.

SOCRATES: So we know that the principle of the uniformity of nature is true only if we know that no miracles happen.

HUME: Yes. The principle is established by experience: a posteriori, not a priori, as you would say.

SOCRATES: And we can know that all those reports are false only if we know that miracles have never happened.

HUME: Yes.

SOCRATES: So we must assume that miracles never occur—in order to prove that miracles never occur. We are begging the question. We are arguing in a circle.

HUME: If you are formulating your argument in that way, yes.

SOCRATES: But that was *your* argument and *your* formulation.

HUME: Perhaps there was a misstep in my way of formulating my argument. Perhaps I should retract what I said about the principle of the uniformity of nature being established by experience. Perhaps I said that too hastily. In fact, perhaps I was right when I denied it in my earlier, longer book, the *Treatise on Human Nature*, when I said that

> **probability is founded on the presumption of a resemblance betwixt those objects of which we have had experience, and those, of which we have had none; and therefore it is impossible** [that] **this presumption can arise from probability.**

SOCRATES: Why do you now think your earlier position was correct, and that you must *assume* or presume the uniformity of nature rather than basing it on experience and probability?

HUME: Because if we did not *assume* the uniformity of nature, our present and past observations would be of no use in calculating the probability of future states of nature resembling past states.

SOCRATES: I think I understand. Could you make it a little clearer and simpler?

HUME: We cannot say that each new experience of natural uniformities and repetitions makes more probable our belief in the uniformity of nature, because we must assume that uniformity in order to have past experience prove anything at all about the probability of future experience. We must assume, rather than prove, that the future will resemble the past.

SOCRATES: I see. That seems clearly correct, especially since we cannot *observe* the future, and observation is the only way to know reality according to your Empiricism.

So how is the principle of the uniformity of nature established then? Is it a matter of fact or a relation of ideas? Is it a mere relation of ideas, true by definition, but not a fact? Or is it a fact and therefore established only by sense observation and repetition of sense observation that makes it more and more probable? We just refuted that alternative, did we not? Is it then a mere relation of ideas, a tautology?

HUME: Suppose it is?

SOCRATES: But the opposite of a tautology is unthinkable. We cannot think that two plus two does not equal five. We cannot write a story about it. We cannot speak meaningfully about it. A world in which 2 + 2 = 4 is not true would be a literally unthinkable, meaningless world. But we *can* think alternatives to the uniformity of nature. By your own standards, miracles are such an alternative, and most men have believed in miracles, and if they believe it, they must think it. You cannot believe something you cannot think at all.

HUME: I do not know how to answer that question. But I do not have to answer that question. I do not have to know how the principle of the uniformity of nature is established. All I need to do is to note that all men do believe in it, whatever the grounds or lack of grounds for that belief. And then, I can appeal to that belief to refute miracles, since miracles are incompatible with it.

SOCRATES: But we have just seen that they are not.

HUME: Because nature digests the miracle, as the earth digests a meteorite?

SOCRATES: Yes.

HUME: Then let us define "miracle" as you do, in terms of its origin. A miracle is caused by God, not by nature, though its effects are digested by nature.

SOCRATES: All right. Now how do you use that definition of miracles to refute the belief in them?

HUME: If we admit that the uniformity of nature is true, for *whatever* reason—for the purposes of my argument now, it does not matter how we establish it, so long as we accept it as true—and if miracles by definition are the exceptions to that rule, and the refutation of that rule, then miracles are by definition false. That is simple logic. For the rule says nature is always uniform and miracles never happen, and miracles say that nature is not always uniform but only most of the time, that is, during those times when miracles are not happening. The universal negative proposition and the particular affirmative proposition contradict each other.

SOCRATES: Of course they do. But if that is your argument, then you are simply saying that miracles do not happen because miracles do not happen. You are begging the question again. You are not considering the evidence, but only the definition.

HUME: But it is a compelling argument. It is logical.

SOCRATES: Only a Rationalist would say that. Your argument against miracles is very much like St. Anselm's argument for God. It has no data, no empirical evidence, as all the good arguments do, both the good arguments against God, like the reality of evil, and the good arguments for God, like causality and design. Similarly, all the good arguments both for and against miracles have data. If you are an Empiricist, that must be your final court of appeal—empirical data. The best argument, scientifically, is the one that best explains the data or explains the most data. Again my suspicion is confirmed: you are not an Empiricist at all but a Rationalist!

HUME: Refute me with a logical argument, not a label.

SOCRATES: All right, then, consider this one: your argument is worthless because its premise and its conclusion are the same proposition in different words. For the two questions "Do miracles happen?" And "Is nature *absolutely* uniform, not just uniform after digesting miracles?" are not two questions at all but only one question in two forms. Your argument then is no argument at all. It simply assumes its own conclusion. It is like saying the number is half a dozen because it is six, or that a certain person is an unmarried man because he is a bachelor.

HUME: So do you say that there is then no role for probability in calculating how likely it is that a reputed miraculous event occurred?

SOCRATES: I do.

HUME: But clearly there is. We use this principle every day.

SOCRATES: Yes we do—with regard to natural events. But not with regard to miracles.

HUME: How arbitrary and unfair and prejudiced!

SOCRATES: Not at all.

HUME: Why not?

SOCRATES: Because a miracle is by definition an event whose cause is supernatural. Did we not agree to that definition?

HUME: Yes.

SOCRATES: Now is a supernatural cause part of nature, or not?

HUME: It is not.

SOCRATES: Then how can a study of probabilities within nature ever tell us how probable it is that God will feed a new event, a supernatural event, into nature? Imagine a fishbowl's. How can the fish in the bowl ever know, from their observations of what happens inside the bowl alone, how probable it is that the creator and maintainer of the fishbowl will put a new item into the fishbowl from outside?

HUME: They could not.

SOCRATES: Unless they knew the fishbowl's creator somehow.

HUME: But they could not know him. They are only fish, and they do not live in his world, or his mind.

SOCRATES: Unless he somehow revealed it to them.

HUME: I see.

SOCRATES: Don't you see that both positions are logically consistent: that there is *not* a fishbowl creator, or at least that he does not miraculously intervene in his fishbowl, and that there *is* such a creator and such miracles.

HUME: It seems so. But surely there is *some* evidence that counts against miracles?

SOCRATES: How? No study of the events in the fishbowl can ever disprove anything outside the fishbowl.

HUME: Or *prove* anything outside the fishbowl.

SOCRATES: No, I think events in the fishbowl *could* possibly prove events outside the fishbowl.

HUME: How?

SOCRATES: They could at least make them more likely, as a fingerprint makes a finger likely.

HUME: But you cannot *prove* miracles by any observation of nature. It is simply a matter of faith.

SOCRATES: No, for if miracles actually happen, it is also a matter of experience and observation.

HUME: But if I have never seen one, it is a matter of faith for me. I must simply choose to believe or not to believe. And the choice not to believe is more rational and more probable.

SOCRATES: You have not shown that it is, and I have refuted your attempt to do so.

HUME: You have only refuted my claim to prove that the principle of the absolute uniformity of nature is more probable than miracles. You have not refuted my claim that it is more probable that those who claim to have seen miracles are lying or hallucinating. Since we all admit, and all agree, that there are many cases of lying or hallucinating, and since we do not all admit, or agree, that miracles happen, it is more probable that people are lying or hallucinating than that miracles actually happen.

SOCRATES: Ah, but here you must consider a very different kind of probability. How probable it is that a certain event will occur in nature can be calculated by statistics or by the laws of physics. But how probable it is that a given person is telling the truth, or lying, or hallucinating, can be reckoned only by another kind of knowledge: the knowledge of his personality, his trustability. And that is such a different kind of knowledge that it has in most languages a different word (though in your poor English language we must use the same word, "know", for both kinds of knowledge: knowledge of events and knowledge of persons).

HUME: Well, I point out that there is good reason to disbelieve the people, and cultures, and religions, that claim miracles. It is credulous people, like the Italians, and credulous times, like the Middle Ages, and credulous religions, like Roman Catholicism, that claim miracles. More enlightened and scientific people, and cultures, and religions do not. As I wrote,

> **It forms a strong presumption against all supernatural and miraculous relations, that they are observed chiefly to abound among ignorant and barbarous nations; or if a civilized people has ever given admission to any of them, that people will be found to have received them from ignorant and barbarous ancestors. . . . Prodigies, omens, oracles, judgements . . . grow thinner every page, in proportion as we advance nearer the enlightened ages.**

E, X, 2

SOCRATES: I have two things to say to this argument. The first is that you are a snob and a racist to assume that the English and especially the Scotch are more trustable than the southern European races. The second is that you again beg the question. For why are these people more trustable and knowledgeable and civilized and enlightened? Because they do not believe in miracles!

HUME: Well, even if my arguments are not conclusive, even if miracles cannot be disproved, they cannot be proved either, so they remain a matter of faith rather than proof. So I am still in a sounder position than the believer. The onus of proof is on him, and he has no proof.

SOCRATES: But who was it that claimed to settle the issue of miracles by proof? It was you. All the believer believes is that they happened, not that he can prove them. You claimed both that they never happened, and that you could prove that they never happened. So the believer is closer to justifying his claim than you are to justifying yours.

HUME: I do not agree that that is so. But even if that is so, I need not believe in miracles. Even if all your arguments are true, I can still be an agnostic and an unbeliever.

SOCRATES: Of course you can.

HUME: Oh. That is a relief. I felt confined and stifled for a minute there. I was afraid I was being given no room to breathe. I have always felt stifled by dogma.

SOCRATES: Do you not think it possible that a believer in miracles, reading your book, would feel stifled by *your* dogma?

HUME: Of course not. That is not possible because I have no dogma.

SOCRATES: Then how do you explain the reaction of the following reader, the one we have quoted before, G. K. Chesterton?

O, IX   Somehow or other an extraordinary idea has arisen that the disbelievers in miracles consider them coldly and fairly, while believers in miracles accept them only in connection with some dogma. The fact is quite the other way. The believers in miracles accept them (rightly or wrongly) because they have evidence for them.

The disbelievers in miracles deny them (rightly or wrongly) because they have a doctrine against them. The open, obvious, democratic thing is to believe an old apple-woman when she bears testimony to a miracle, just as you believe an old apple-woman when she bears testimony to a murder. . . . If it comes to human testimony there is a choking cataract of human testimony in favour of the supernatural. If you reject it, you can only mean one of two things. You reject the peasant's story about the ghost either because the man is a peasant or because the story is a ghost story. That is, you either deny the main principle of democracy, or you affirm the main principle of materialism—the abstract impossibility of miracle. You have a perfect right to do so; but in that case you are the dogmatist. . . . If I say "a peasant saw a ghost," I am told, "But peasants are so credulous." If I ask, "Why credulous?" the only answer is—that they see ghosts.

HUME: I grant that that form of argument reasons in a circle. But that is not my argument.

SOCRATES: It seems to be one of them.

HUME: Not the main one.

SOCRATES: But we have already refuted the main one, and we are now considering your later one, the fact of all the fake miracles.

HUME: Yes, let's consider that. What about all the fake miracles? Everyone must admit that there are many, many cases of claimed miracles, or apparent miracles, that have been proved to be fake by a scientific method; but there have been no cases of miracles that have been proved by the scientific method. As I wrote,

E, X, 2   **The many instances of forged miracles, and prophecies, and supernatural events, which, in all ages, have either been detected by contrary evidence, or which detect themselves by their absurdity, prove sufficiently the strong propensity of mankind to the extraordinary and the marvellous, and ought reasonably to beget a suspicion against all relations of this kind.**

SOCRATES: So you think that admitting the existence of many fake miracles counts against the existence of any true ones?

HUME: Of course.

SOCRATES: I should think it counts for the opposite.

HUME: What? Why?

SOCRATES: If there is a lot of counterfeit money, does this count against belief in the existence of some real money, or for it?

HUME: Logically, it counts for it.

SOCRATES: More than that, even: it *presupposes* the existence of real money.

HUME: By definition, yes. But that proves nothing regarding matters of fact and existence. Are you finished now?

SOCRATES: Not quite. There is one other question I have. I wonder about your *strategy*, so to speak, and your *motives* in this attack on miracles. I find something very puzzling here. For on the one hand, you dismiss miracles as irrational, but on the other hand you say that Christianity is not *supposed* to be rational! So why are you scandalized by miracles?

HUME: Where do I say that Christianity is not supposed to be rational? What are my exact words and what are you puzzled about in them?

SOCRATES: I am thinking of the following passage, and, frankly, I am puzzled about whether you were sincere or not when you wrote it:

> **I am . . . pleased with the method of reason-**   E, X, 1
> **ing here delivered** [the critique of miracles], **as**
> **I think it may serve to confound those dan-**
> **gerous friends or disguised enemies to the**
> ***Christian Religion*, who have undertaken to**
> **defend it by the principles of human reason.**
> **Our most holy religion is founded on *Faith*,**
> **not on reason; and it is a sure method of ex-**
> **posing it to put it to such a trial as it is, by**
> **no means, fitted to endure.**

I can make no sense of this passage except the following paraphrase:

"Those who prove by reason that Christianity is true are not friends of Christianity but enemies. Christianity cannot be defended by reason. It is irrational. If you think rationally, you cannot prove it to be true, but you *can* prove it is false. If you dare to expose it to thought, you will refute it as a silly fairy tale. But we believe it anyway."

Everything up to the last sentence of that paraphrase is exactly what an atheist would say. There is only one reason I can imagine why a man as rational and intelligent as you would ever say that last sentence: you *are* an atheist but you hide this because you fear losing your job, your reputation, your income, or your friends.

HUME: But whatever my personal motives may have been, the fact is that Christianity is not based on reason. It is based on faith.

SOCRATES: Whether it is based on faith, or reason, or both, or neither, it is certainly based on Jesus, is it not?

HUME: Of course.

SOCRATES: And in the Gospels Jesus always gave reasons.

HUME: But His Father did not. The God of the Old Testament is arbitrary.

SOCRATES: Not so. He says, "Come now, let us reason together." He *always* has good reasons for what He does, according to that book. Frankly, I wonder whether you ever read it. You seem to confuse God with Zeus. It is Zeus that is arbitrary, not the God of the Bible.

HUME: Well, whatever God may be, Christianity isn't a rational philosophy. It's a faith.

SOCRATES: So you say faith and reason contradict each other.

HUME: Of course.

SOCRATES: So you are not a Christian.

HUME: I am.

SOCRATES: You cannot be all three of these things: a rational, logical, intelligent man, *and* a Christian, *and* one who believes that Christian faith and reason contradict each other.

HUME: Why not?

SOCRATES: Because if you are intelligent and logical, you will see that saying that Christian faith and reason contradict each other is saying that Christianity is disproved by reason. And if it is disproved, then it is proved to be false, and if it is proved to be false, then it is false. And if you believe it is false, you are not a Christian.

HUME: Are there Inquisitors right behind you, Socrates?

SOCRATES: I am not surprised that you would think that. No, we have no such nonsense here. You are required only to be honest, not orthodox.

HUME: Do you mean that?

SOCRATES: I do.

HUME: Oh.

SOCRATES: You seem surprised.

HUME: Perhaps it is true after all: perhaps there is a Heaven—a place of justice and light and reason. And perhaps it is here.

SOCRATES: And perhaps there is even a God of justice and light and reason!

HUME: If so, perhaps I was wrong when I criticized so many things in this religion.

SOCRATES: That is what I want to investigate next: the other Christian doctrines that you argue against, in addition to miracles.

11

Hume's Critiques of Christianity

SOCRATES: We have already looked at your critique of miracles, and of the synthesis of faith and reason, that is, of the traditional Christian claim that faith and reason do not contradict each other. There are quite a few other important ideas taught by Christianity that you criticize: that man has free will; that his soul and his reason are different in kind from the souls and reason of animals; and even that man *has* a soul, or self. Not in this book but in others, you critique the very existence of the self because the self is a substance (a being, an entity), and you critique the notion of "substance" as not in principle empirically observable. Also, you criticize the idea that God exercises what you call "particular providence" over human life—that, as Jesus claimed, not a hair falls from our head without the will of the Father. For this too, of course, is not empirically verifiable. You also criticize the notion that there is what you call "a future state", or life after death. To this list of endangered ideas we may add the very idea of God Himself, for you argue, in your *Dialogues on Natural Religion*,[1] that

---

[1] Texts quoted from Hume's *Dialogues on Natural Religion* are indicated as DNR in the sidenotes.

DNR,   **Our ideas reach no further than our expe-**
§2,   **rience. We have no experience of divine at-**
para. 4   **tributes and operations. I need not conclude**
           my syllogism. You can draw the inference
           yourself.

Your reputation as an enemy of the Christian faith is based not only on (1) your famous critique of miracles and (2) your denial that Christianity is rational, but also on these six additional issues that I have mentioned, plus the reduction of morality to emotion. Put these nine issues together and you can see why most readers concluded, perhaps not without reason, that you were an atheist. How is it meaningful to call you a Christian if you deny

1. that miracles ever happen—thus no creation, prophets, Incarnation, Resurrection, or Second Coming;
2. that Christianity can endure rational critique;
3. that we have free will;
4. that man is anything more than a clever ape;
5. that there is such a thing as the soul;
6. that there is such a thing as divine providence, that God knows and cares and loves us;
7. that there is life after death;
8. that the concept of God is an idea with any meaning;
9. and that morality is anything more than subjective feeling?

HUME: It does not follow from these denials that I was an atheist. I nowhere argue against the existence of God, only against the validity of the traditional metaphysical arguments for Him and His attributes.

SOCRATES: You are an agnostic, then?

HUME: If the word means one who neither believes nor disbelieves, I would reject that term too. I am willing to be called a believer. I just believe that believing is quite different from knowing, and very different from proving.

SOCRATES: I do not understand how you can say you believe in something if you do not know anything at all about that thing. What content would your belief have?

HUME: It has content. I just do not think it can be proved.

SOCRATES: Where do you derive the content?

HUME: From the teachings of my church, the Church of England.

SOCRATES: Then why do you disagree with nine of the most important points of that content, if not because you claim to know that reason has disproved them?

HUME: Because I believe that. Reason has a veto power over faith. Most of us freethinkers believe that, though I do not think ordinary believers will accept that idea.

SOCRATES: On the contrary, it is a familiar and traditional idea that reason has a veto power over faith, if what you mean by that is simply that no honest person can believe what reason has refuted.

For instance, St. Thomas Aquinas implicitly teaches this. For this point would seem to follow logically with necessity from the simple premise that Christianity is true.

HUME: How would that follow?

SOCRATES: If Christianity is true, then there can never be a single contradiction between any doctrine of the Christian faith and any proposition proved to be true by reason, whether in science or in history or in common sense or anywhere else. For what is proved true is true, and truth does not contradict truth; so if Christianity is true, it contradicts no other truth and is contradicted by no other truth.

HUME: I suppose that logically follows.

SOCRATES: And do you see what else follows, with regard to proofs?

HUME: What?

SOCRATES: That whenever there is any rational argument against any Christian doctrine, that argument can be refuted in a purely logical way, without assuming or using or relying on any religious doctrine. It can be refuted by finding in it either a logical fallacy, or a false premise, or an ambiguous term.

HUME: That would seem to be a bold conclusion. I do not see how this bold claim logically follows simply from the belief that Christianity is true.

SOCRATES: Oh, but it does, quite clearly. For if this "bold claim", as you call it, is *not* true—this "bold claim" that *every* argument against every Christian doctrine can be refuted in a purely logical way—

why, then there is at least one argument that can *not* be logically refuted. Does that not follow?

HUME: Yes. And that is what I believe.

SOCRATES: And an argument that cannot be refuted is an argument that has no logical fallacy, no false premise, and no ambiguous term, correct?

HUME: Correct.

SOCRATES: And an argument that has no logical fallacy, no false premise, and no ambiguous term is an argument that proves what?

HUME: It proves its conclusion to be true.

SOCRATES: Exactly. And if a conclusion can be proved to be true, then it is in fact what?

HUME: If it is validly proved to be true, then it is in fact true.

SOCRATES: Exactly. And if it is true, then its contradictory must be what?

HUME: False.

SOCRATES: Quite so. But what is its contradictory?

HUME: Its contradictory is some doctrine of Christianity. That is what the argument was trying to disprove.

SOCRATES: Correct. Well, if it succeeded in doing this thing that it was trying to do, then what did it disprove?

HUME: Christianity.

SOCRATES: Yes. So in that case, then, it proved Christianity to be false—in this one doctrine, at least. And you cannot believe as true what you believe to be false!

HUME: That sounds perfectly clear and simple and logical. But perhaps things are not in fact so clear and simple and logical. Perhaps science and religion contradict each other and yet both are true in some way.

SOCRATES: In what way? Are you taking refuge in some esoteric mysticism now? Or some kind of Subjectivism?

HUME: Why do you say that?

SOCRATES: Because when you say that you believe that reason has a veto power over faith, you seem to mean something more than traditional Christians mean. They mean that since truth cannot contradict truth, if Christianity is true then it can never be proved to be false. But you seem to mean that it *can*. At least in these nine ideas that I have listed. But if you say that Christianity can be proved to be false, but you believe it anyway, you are saying that you believe it is false *and* that you believe it is true.

HUME: That is not what I am saying.

SOCRATES: I hope not. By definition, truth cannot contradict truth. Only falsehood contradicts truth. Don't you remember your logic?

HUME: Not with as much trust as you do, I think.

SOCRATES: What do you mean by that?

HUME: I mean that I do not think reason has as much power in human thought as you think it has. And I do not think that most Christians think it has, either.

SOCRATES: That does not refute my argument.

HUME: Why not?

SOCRATES: Would you not say that logic is like a sword?—an instrument for accomplishing an end?

HUME: It is that, among other things.

SOCRATES: And suppose a child were to take a strong, sharp sword and use it clumsily and not well. Would that mean that there was anything wrong or weak with the sword itself?

HUME: No.

SOCRATES: And are we humans not often like children when it comes to using the powerful tools of logic? Do we not often err?

HUME: Of course.

SOCRATES: So the fact that *we* are not perfectly logical does not mean that logic is not perfectly logical.

HUME: I quite agree.

SOCRATES: But if this is so, then whether or not there is any contradiction between the Christian faith and reason, there clearly *is* a contradiction between what *you* say about the relation between religious faith and logical reason, and what Christianity says about it. You say Christianity is irrational and refutable, and they say it is not.

HUME: I do not agree that Christianity says this. You say it, and St. Thomas says it, and Catholics say it, and tradition says it, but modern, enlightened Christians do not say it.

SOCRATES: And I am trying to get in focus just what you "modern, enlightened Christians" do say about faith and reason.

HUME: We say something different than traditional Christians say. We are suspicious of the possibility of a marriage between faith and reason. We do not think they are marriable. We think they are like a cat and a dog. So I suppose this will just have to count as one of the nine disagreements that you listed between my philosophy and that of traditional Christianity. I am not loath to admit such disagreements, for I have clearly done so with regard to miracles. Will you now subject my other disagreements with Christian teaching that you mentioned to a similar investigation too, as you have done with miracles?

SOCRATES: That would require a very long investigation. We have already spent far more time on the question of miracles than on any other question in your book, because of its practical interest, because of the difference it makes. And there are many other important religious issues raised in this little book of yours. For instance, the issue of free will in Section VIII, "Of Liberty and Necessity", and the issue of the distinction between man and animals in Section IX, "Of the Reason of Animals", and the ideas of divine providence and life after death in Section XI, "Of a particular Providence and of a future State".

HUME: So will you examine these sections now too?

SOCRATES: I think I will not.

HUME: Why not?

SOCRATES: Because it is only that your critique of miracles has lasted and has been influential.

HUME: But what if these other critiques are equally deserving of such fame?

SOCRATES: They are not. And that is my second reason for not exploring them. There is a good reason why your critique of miracles has become famous but the others have not. The reason is that your critique of miracles is quite clear and logical, and easy to analyze. The reader knows he can get his mind around it. And this is also true of your attack upon objective morality, which Christianity has also always affirmed and which you deny. And that is why I included that, briefly, in this investigation, but NOT these other four issues. For frankly, the sections on these four issues are so hard for me to get clear in my mind that I feel like a tired professor faced with a student paper whose argument he finds hard to evaluate because he finds it hard to detect them. It feels like trying to operate on an animal that you have not yet captured.

HUME: Oh, thank you for your clear and logical evaluation, Socrates!

SOCRATES: When I see a clear and logical argument, I will undertake a clear and logical evaluation. I would, however, briefly like to explore the *consequences* of these denials. I would like to explore what kind of religion you have left if you deny these nine things, and whether this religion could in any way still be called Christianity. For that is a question simply of logic, or definition, of clear meanings. And that is my thing, so to speak. So I wonder what is left of Christianity when all the miracles I mentioned and all nine of these doctrines are subtracted?

HUME: This is left: that Jesus existed, and lived, and taught, and that he was a man of marvelous wisdom, and that he is a worthy figure to center the world's greatest religion around, for he practiced what he preached. He taught and showed all the virtues.

SOCRATES: Like any saint, rabbi, prophet, mystic, moralist, or philosopher. Like Buddha, or Solomon, or Confucius, or Lao Tzu, or Muhammad.

HUME: Yes.

SOCRATES: But how is that in any way distinctively Christian, if he is the same sort of thing as all these others?

HUME: I thought we were supposed to discuss what I wrote, not what I did not write. That is not the point of my book.

SOCRATES: But your book *is* about some of the claims of Christianity, and Christianity is about your beliefs and your soul.

HUME: I thought we were investigating my book, not my soul.

SOCRATES: True. The other investigation will come soon enough. Let us return to our humbler task, then.

12

Hume's Denial of the Self

SOCRATES: The reason I asked the deeper question, the more personal question about your soul, was not to usurp the deeper personal judgment that you will soon face, but because I did not understand the logic of your position on faith and reason. In fact I still do not understand just what you believe and why you call it Christianity. I wanted you to define your terms, that's all.

And now, though I am investigating your philosophy and not your soul, I would like to briefly investigate your philosophy of the soul, or your denial that there *is* a soul or self at all. I want to do this for philosophical reasons, as well as for personal reasons.

HUME: What personal reasons?

SOCRATES: Well, if you have no self, then you have no reasons to fear any judgment upon it, but if you do—well, then. . . . But as I said, that is not *my* area of competence. I judge only your ideas, and you do have the idea that there is no self behind your ideas.

HUME: But I made this point not in this book, the *Enquiry*, but in my earlier, longer *Treatise on Human Nature*.

SOCRATES: Yes, but we should investigate it, because the notion of no soul is almost as notorious as your critique of miracles or your critique of causality. It would seem to be a startling idea: that there is no such thing as self, or ego, or what we mean by "I". The thing Descartes thought most certain, you declare not only uncertain but unknowable, and not only unknowable but nonexistent! And you arrive at this conclusion not by mystical experience, as Buddha did, but by rational *thought*. So instead of Descartes' "I think, therefore I am", you say: "I think that I am not"!

HUME: I am willing to defend my controversial idea, even though it is not in the book under investigation.

SOCRATES: Good. Here, then, are your words from that other book, your *Treatise on Human Nature*. It is a very complex and clever argument:

THN,
VI
There are some philosophers, who imagine we are every moment intimately conscious of what we call our *self*; that we feel its existence and its continuance in existence, and are certain, beyond the evidence of a demonstration, both of its perfect identity and simplicity. . . .

Unluckily, all these positive assertions are contrary to that very experience which is pleaded for them, nor have we any idea of *self*, after the manner it is here explained.

For from what impression could this idea be derived? This question it is impossible to answer without a manifest contradiction and absurdity; and yet it is a question which must

necessarily be answered, if we would have the idea of self pass for clear and intelligible. It must be some one impression, that gives rise to every real idea. But self or person is not any one impression, but that to which our several impressions and ideas are supposed to have a reference. If any impression gives rise to the idea of self, that impression must continue invariably the same, through the whole course of our lives; since self is supposed to exist after that manner. But there is no impression constant and invariable. Pain and pleasure, grief and joy, passions and sensations succeed each other, and never all exist at the same time. It cannot, therefore, be from any of these impressions, or from any other, that the idea of [the] self is derived; and consequently there is no such idea.

HUME: I hope you understand, Socrates, that this argument must be taken in the context of my general critique of substance, for if the very idea of substance is unknowable, and if the self is a substance (a spiritual substance), then this is the quickest and simplest argument to prove the conclusion that the self is unknowable.

SOCRATES: I do understand that. Let us examine this "quick argument" first. It is stated nicely by Robert Pirsig in a book that says some nice things about you. It has the strange title of *Zen and the Art of Motorcycle Maintenance*,[1] but it is more philosophical than its

---

[1] Pirsig, Robert M. *Zen and the Art of Motorcycle Maintenance: An Inquiry into Values* (New York: Bantam, 1981).

title. Pirsig summarizes your argument against substance this way: "Since all knowledge comes from sensory impressions and since no sensory impression of substance itself, it follows logically that there's no knowledge of substance."

HUME: That is a fair summary of my main argument.

SOCRATES: Are you sure you do not want to modify Pirsig's version of it?

HUME: No, that expresses what I want to say quite well.

SOCRATES: Then I am afraid I will have to tax you with an elementary fallacy in logic.

HUME: Which one?

SOCRATES: The Fallacy of Four Terms. In fact, I count *five*. For you argue that: Since all knowledge comes from sensory impressions (premise one) And since there is no sensory impression of substance itself (premise two), Therefore it follows logically that there is no knowledge of substance (conclusion).

So, All (knowledge) is (something that comes from sensory impressions) And no (substance) is (that of which there is a sensory impression) Therefore no (substance) is (that of which there is knowledge).

HUME: I see it, Socrates. "*That of which* there is knowledge" and "knowledge" seem to be two different terms. And the same with "sensory impression" and "*that of which* there is a sensory impression."

SOCRATES: So you see your fallacy.

HUME: Yes, but I can patch it up easily. I can identify the two disparate terms, knowledge and its object, and I can do the same with the two terms "sensory impressions" and their object, and thus reduce the five terms to three.

SOCRATES: How?

HUME: By a simple principle of epistemology: that in all true knowledge, the content of the thing known and the content of the knowledge must be identical. For if the content of the knowledge (or the sensory impression) and the content of the real object of which there is knowledge (or sensory impression) are *not* identical, then the knowledge (or sensory impression) is not true. So these two terms—knowledge and its object (and also sense impressions and their object)—are not different in content, but identical. You see, I mean by "knowledge" the *content* of knowledge, which is identical with the real thing known, if the knowledge is true; and I mean by "sensory impression" the *content* of sensory impression, which is identical with the real thing sensed, if the sense impression is true. So there are only three terms, not five. We can just subtract the words "that of which there is".

SOCRATES: I see some problems with that.

HUME: What?

SOCRATES: For one thing, you seem to be confusing, or wrongly identifying, the *object* of knowledge or sensation with the *content* of knowledge or sensation.

HUME: What is the difference?

SOCRATES: The object is the whole real entity or event known or sensed: a hurricane, for instance. But the content is only those aspects of the real object that we happen to know or sense. Unless you are God and know everything in the real object, the content is always less than the object. And that is how they differ.

HUME: Suppose I speak only of contents and not of real objects at all. Let us simply subtract the "that of which".

SOCRATES: Alas, even then there are still four terms in your argument rather than three.

HUME: How do you get to that conclusion?

SOCRATES: This way: if we subtract the words "that of which there is", as you say, then your argument looks like this:

— All (knowledge) is (that which comes from a sensory impression).

— And no (substance) is (a sensory impression).

— Therefore no (substance) is (knowledge).

You can see the four terms here. For "that which *comes from* a sensory impression" may not be the same as "sensory impression".

HUME: What do you see as the difference between a sensory impression, or the content of a sensory impression, and "that which comes from" it?

SOCRATES: Well, one possibility would be this: in Aristotle's philosophy, universal ideas come from sensory impressions by a process of abstraction—we know humanness, the universal form, by abstracting it from the sensory impression of many humans, and we know the universal form we call greenness by abstracting it from the sensory impressions of this green grass and that green tie and so forth. But we never have a sensory impression of an abstract universal, only of a concrete particular.

HUME: Oh. Well, I was not thinking of Aristotle when I wrote that. I should be more careful and complete. I will refute Aristotle's doctrine of universals and abstraction in my next book.

SOCRATES: Alas, there is no more time for writing new books, only for understanding and defending (or repenting of) old ones. You are dead, you know. This is not earth, this is Purgatory.

HUME: Oh.

SOCRATES: And what you wrote on earth must be examined, for it imperils not just one doctrine (namely, the knowledge of universals by abstraction) in one division of philosophy (namely, epistemology) in one ancient philosopher (namely, Aristotle), but it imperils the very enterprise of philosophy itself.

HUME: Why? I was a philosopher.

SOCRATES: Yes, but you were a suicidal philosopher. Your philosophy was the suicide of philosophy. If your philosophy were true, then it would not be true, for if your philosophy were true, then no philosophy could be true, including yours.

HUME: Because of my skepticism?

SOCRATES: Yes, because of your skepticism, and also because of this particular skeptical point, that there is no self. For if I was right about philosophy, it is our response to the divine command "Know thyself." But if there is no self, then there is no self to know, and we cannot know the self and thus cannot philosophize. So we must conclude by examining this most crucial point, your "bottom line" conclusion of skepticism.

13

Hume's Skepticism

SOCRATES: You must have realized that you would be famous above all for your skepticism, for that is where you end your book, that is your final conclusion. You also reserve your most memorable and striking paragraph for the very end, the deservedly famous attack on traditional nonskeptical philosophy:

> **When we run over libraries, persuaded of these principles, what havoc must we make? If we take in our hand any volume; of divinity or school metaphysics, for instance; let us ask:** *Does it contain any abstract reasoning concerning quantity or number?* **No.** *Does it contain any experimental reasoning concerning matter of fact and existence?* **No. Commit it then to the flames: for it can contain nothing but sophistry and illusion.**

E, XII, 3

HUME: A great passage, isn't it? I'll bet it haunted the dreams of many philosophers who read it.

SOCRATES: Indeed it did. But what we must investigate now is whether or not this very attack on traditional philosophy as "sophistry and illusion" is or is not itself an example of sophistry and illusion.

HUME: Examine away, Socrates!

SOCRATES: My first question is this: I wonder whether you mean this conclusion literally.

HUME: Suppose I do?

SOCRATES: In that case, I wonder how much of pre-Humean philosophy would be burnt?

HUME: Most of it.

SOCRATES: And post-Humean philosophy too.

HUME: Let it be so.

SOCRATES: And even this conversation!

HUME: I am perfectly willing to erase this conversation!

SOCRATES: Would any ethics or metaphysics or theology survive?

HUME: Apparently not.

SOCRATES: I think you are aware that most readers will regard this not as your triumphant summit but as your suicide, as your *reductio ad absurdum*.

HUME: The fact that people are shocked and upset by an idea does not constitute a refutation or even an evaluation of it.

SOCRATES: Quite so. So let us evaluate.

HUME: On what principles?

SOCRATES: Your own. To evaluate your skepticism, let us turn to your earlier section, Section V, "Skeptical Solution of these Doubts", as well as your lastsection, Section XII, "Of the academical or skeptical Philosophy", where you lay down your principles and your definitions of skepticism.

HUME: Fine.

SOCRATES: Let me begin by asking you what, exactly, you mean by skepticism. For the demand to define our terms at the beginning is really a demand to be fair.

HUME: Thank you for that fairness. I distinguish my "Academic skepticism" from that of the old Greek skeptics who followed Phyrro, the "Phyrronian skeptics". Phyrronian skepticism was a simple and total skepticism of all doctrines, all teachings, all claims to truth. Now *that* claim is immediately self-contradictory, of course, for it is a claim to know that we can know nothing, a claim to know the truth about our inability to know the truth.

SOCRATES: I'm happy to hear you say that. We can get that silly and self-contradictory idea out of the way, then.

HUME: But my skepticism is a reasonable skepticism. It is a *probabilism*. It affirms probable knowledge of matters of fact. It denies only dogmatic certainty. Its principle is the demand that we proportion our belief to the evidence, and since all our evidence about matter of fact and existence, as distinct from "relations of ideas" in mathematics, is only probable, it therefore maintains that we have only various degrees of probable knowledge.

SOCRATES: Are you certain of your probabilism? Or is your probabilism itself only probable?

HUME: Clearly, I would involve myself in the same sort of self-contradiction as we found in simple Phyrrhonian skepticism if I said that I was certain that I was not certain but had only probabilities.

SOCRATES: So probabilism is itself only probable?

HUME: Yes.

SOCRATES: So a doubt remains about that too, a "perhaps"—perhaps probabilism is not true, but false, or perhaps it is not merely probable, but certain.

HUME: Perhaps.

SOCRATES: Why then are you so passionately opposed to the claim to certainty if it may "perhaps" be true? That sounds very dogmatic!

HUME: It is a methodology, not a conclusion. I am skeptical as you were, Socrates: I subject every idea to critique, just as you do.

SOCRATES: Oh, I don't think so.

HUME: You mean I failed to critique some of my presuppositions?

SOCRATES: That too, yes. But what I meant was that I do not think your skepticism matched mine at all.

HUME: Because mine is a doctrine as well as a method, a conclusion as well as a starting point?

SOCRATES: That too, yes.

HUME: I think you have not yet refuted my conclusion.

SOCRATES: I think I have. But let me try again. Here is a very simple argument against your probabilism:

universal probabilism is self-contradictory because to know the probable, you must know the certain. For let us suppose that every proposition about matters of fact is only probable. Let us call some such proposition x. Then not only is x only probable—for instance that the sun will rise tomorrow—but it is also only probable that it is only probable that the sun will rise tomorrow. Let us call that proposition y. If y is a proposition, and if all propositions are only probable, then y also is only probable. And then the proposition that says that y is only probable—let us call that proposition z—is also only probable.

HUME: And we have infinite regress. So what? That is not a problem. There are legitimate infinite regresses, such as we have in the number series: we can always add another integer. So here we add a question to every proposition, including the infinite series of propositions about other propositions. We can do the same with truths: if a is true, then b, which says that a is true, is also true; and so is c, which says that b is true, et cetera et cetera ad infinitum. If there is no problem with an infinite regress of true propositions, there is no problem with an infinite regress of probable propositions.

SOCRATES: But the two cases are different. We know that a is true before we know that b is true, but we do not know whether x is probable or not until we know y. For y tells us that x is probable. And we do not know whether y is probable or not until we know z. So if the series or propositions is infinite, we do not ever know that x is probable. It is like an infinite regress of causes: if there is no uncaused cause, no first cause, then there can be no second causes, for subsequent causes depend on prior causes. So you must posit some "first cause", so to speak, some certainly true proposition that tells you with certainty that the other propositions are probably true.

HUME: No, there is a way out of your dilemma, Socrates. For if all propositions are only probable, and if x, y, and z are propositions, then they are all only probable. And if the series of propositions is infinite, then they are all only probable.

SOCRATES: But then you are using deduction, not induction. You are deducing that x, y, and z are only probable from your general principle that all propositions are only probable.

HUME: So what?

SOCRATES: How do you know this general principle, this universal truth, if you are a Nominalist and do not believe in real universals?

HUME: Oh. Well, we must make exceptions somewhere.

SOCRATES: That is hardly an adequate answer to the charge of self-contradiction.

HUME: You misunderstand the point of my skepticism, Socrates. It is not a theoretical point but a practical one. It is a counsel, a method. That is why I claim it is your skepticism too. It is a moral philosophy, not a theoretical philosophy.

SOCRATES: In other words, it is a good thing to do, to be skeptical.

HUME: Yes. It is good.

SOCRATES: But not true.

HUME: No, not true. Good.

SOCRATES: How suddenly you withdraw the claim that it is true! Well, let us examine that other claim, then, that skepticism is good, and moral. Why do you say it is?

HUME: As I wrote, skepticism is a moral philosophy because it fosters **no disorderly passion of the human mind.** Skepticism is the enemy of the vices of credulity and sloth, which are disorderly passions of the mind. I'm sure you agree with that.   E, V, 1

SOCRATES: I agree that the passion to believe the unbelievable, the laziness that refuses to question, and the fear that refuses to doubt, are indeed "disorderly passions of the human mind". But do you not think that the passion to doubt and attack and refute and refuse an idea even when that idea is true and rational and provable and not reasonably doubtable—do you not think that this is also a disorderly passion?

HUME: Of course. But the passion to doubt the doubtable, to refute the refutable, is an orderly passion, not a disorderly passion.

SOCRATES: True.

HUME: So it all depends on whether the ideas I doubt and refute in coming to my skeptical conclusion are indeed doubtable and refutable—in other words, whether my arguments for skepticism are valid. If they are, then my skepticism is not disorderly. If they are not, it is.

SOCRATES: Nothing could be clearer.

HUME: And they are valid if they prove the conclusion they claim to prove.

SOCRATES: Of course.

HUME: Not some other conclusion that they do not claim to prove.

SOCRATES: Of course.

HUME: I think, then, that we should be very clear about just what conclusion I claim to prove. I have been unfairly maligned as a destructive skeptic, a total skeptic, a foolish skeptic; and I need to show you the difference between that kind of skepticism and my kind, which is constructive, not destructive, and is only partial and not total, and wise rather than foolish. That is the difference between Academic skepticism and Phyrronian skepticism. And what this difference means, I state very clearly:

E, V, 1   **The academics always talk of doubt and suspense of judgement, of danger in hasty determinations, of confining to very narrow bounds the enquiries of the understanding, and of renouncing all speculations which lie not within the limits of common life and practice. Nothing, therefore, can be more contrary than such a philosophy to the supine indolence of the mind, its rash arrogance, its lofty pretensions, and its superstitious credulity. Every passion is mortified by it, except the love of truth. . . . It is surprising, therefore, that this philosophy, which, in al-**

most every instance, must be harmless and innocent, should be the subject of so much groundless reproach and obloquy . . . of [its] enemies, who stigmatize it as libertine, profane, and irreligious.

SOCRATES: I think I see one thing very clearly, David. I do *not* see clearly whether you are in fact a prejudiced, irrational, ideological, a priori enemy of religion or not; but I *do* see clearly that you do not *believe* you are that and that you do not *want* to be that.

HUME: You see my heart and not just my head. Thank you.

SOCRATES: Others probably judge you to have a clever and adequate head—perhaps a *too* adequate head—but a hard and defective heart. I do not see you that way. I see you as having a less adequate head than you seem to have, but also as having a more adequate heart than you seem to have.

HUME: I do not know whether to thank you for this judgment, and be flattered, or to be insulted and to dispute it.

SOCRATES: I think that is the most charming thing you have said yet. And the wisest.

HUME: Why?

SOCRATES: Because it is the humblest. It began with the magic words "I do not know".

HUME: Your favorite words, Socrates! You compliment me only when I resemble yourself.

SOCRATES: I am sorry if that is how I appear to you. Can you not entertain the possibility that my standard is not myself but truth? That I am not a tyrant but a teacher?

HUME: If you are a teacher, what have you tried to teach me? What was your goal in all this dialogue? What did you hope to accomplish by it?

SOCRATES: I hope to have taught you at least just a little of the first and most important lessons I have ever learned. I call it my Lesson One. It is the lesson of intellectual humility, that we know far less than we seem to know. That is *my* "skepticism".

HUME: But that is exactly the lesson I also tried to teach mankind! That is why I am a skeptic! The only difference, as you said before, is that we began there but I also ended there. I ended with a more nearly universal skepticism than you did.

SOCRATES: No, I think it is the opposite. I think I was more universally skeptical than you were.

HUME: What a surprising thing to say! Why?

SOCRATES: Because you were not skeptical of your skepticism, as I was.

HUME: Perhaps you are right about that.

SOCRATES: I see you are learning Lesson One after all!

HUME: But my *motive* for skepticism, at the beginning, was the same as yours, I think. And we both concluded with at least some skepticism. So I do resemble you, though not completely. Is it not therefore ironic and unjust that I am judged and condemned by you because of my resemblance to you?

SOCRATES: At every point of my critique of your philosophy, we found a deep *difference*, not a similarity.

HUME: Between your mind and my mind, perhaps. But not between your intentions and mine.

SOCRATES: I cannot judge your intentions. Only Another can. And soon will. I have judged only your arguments. Or, rather, Reason has judged your arguments. I have endeavored only to be Reason's instrument.